THE LEARNING ENCOUNTER

The Classroom
as a Communications Workshop

Margaret L. Clark,
Queens College

Ella A. Erway,
Southern Connecticut State College

Lee Beltzer,
Brooklyn College

CONSULTING EDITOR: Russel Windes, *Queens College*

THE LEARNING ENCOUNTER

The Classroom as a Communications Workshop

RANDOM HOUSE
New York

Photo Acknowledgments

Fig. 4–1: Photo by Stuart Leventhal
Fig. 4–2: Courtesy of United Press International
Fig. 4–3: Photo by Georgeen Comerford
Fig. 4–4: Photo by B. Patchowsky
Fig. 4–5: Photo by Stuart Leventhal
Fig. 4–6: Photo by Stuart Leventhal
Fig. 4–7: Photo by Dennis Chalkin for the New York Times Magazine

Part Title Acknowledgments

Phases 1,
2 and 3: From *the me nobody knows: children's voices from the ghetto*,
edited by Stephen M. Joseph.
Copyright © 1969 by Stephen M. Joseph.
Reprinted by permission of Avon Books, Mr. Joseph, and his agents,
Henry Morrison, Inc. (see pp. 3, 35, 77).
Phase 4: Copyright © 1967, Northern Songs Limited. Used by permission.
All Rights Reserved.

ISBN: 0–394–31161–2

Library of Congress Catalog Card Number: 78–146905

Manufactured in the United States of America. Composed, printed, and bound by The
H. Wolff Book Mfg. Co., Inc., New York, N.Y.

First Edition
9 8 7 6 5 4 3 2 1

To
Robert Sheffield Clark

Preface

The authors of the following pages are not prescribing a formula for flawless teaching or a panacea for the many problems of the classroom. Rather, we are offering a set of parameters for viewing student/teacher relationships and for teaching interpersonal communication with the hope of opening up new vistas and stimulating student and teacher to extend their thinking, to probe their potential for cooperative creativity. We are suggesting that the old lecture format for presenting material be put aside and that the emphasis be put upon how the student deals with substantive material rather than how he retains it. In place of stressing a student's ability to recall notes, we would prefer that the student be forced to make some decisions about ideas and the utilization of data. With this in mind we feel that we will have failed if students should ever be tested in the traditional question-answer manner on the material in this text.

Our communication-oriented classroom is one in which the students and teachers function as a single unit with a single purpose—to learn how to relate to each other effectively both as encoders and decoders. Encoding and decoding are not examined as simple means of carrying information from one source to another as if words were used merely to carry content. Rather, we look upon every interchange as defining the relationship between the sources as well as conveying information. The systems analysis was chosen because it allows for the isolation of many factors involved in communication and because it captures the dynamic and elusive qualities of the communicative act. Above all, the systemic analysis dramatizes the irreversible quality of the communication encounter: No word said can be unsaid; no action can be undone. The systems model takes this into account and underscores the necessity for our classroom society to be open to change and adjust accordingly.

Even our most highly regarded schools are suddenly feeling the stress of student pressure, and many will be surprised to find that the problems we consider central to the inner-city school apply as well to affluent suburban communities:

> The kids of Winnetka are not really allowed to find the skills that fit their needs. They are forced to think they must accept those of their parents. Those skills may have worked for food gathering and hunting societies, but existence in this one is problematic at best for entirely other reasons than physical needs. Survival now is primarily an intellectual and emotional struggle, of creating different fantasies, different dreams.[1]

To some the outlook may seem gloomy. But if one looks at the environment and sees the virility of young, committed students, he can overcome his pessimism with a sense of anticipation and excitement about the possibilities that lie before students and teachers if we are willing to break down the old barriers and build new relationships.

February 1971   M. L. C.
                                                                 E. A. E.
                                                                 L. B.

[1] Wallace Roberts, "No Place to Grow," *Saturday Review,* March 21, 1970, p. 80.

Acknowledgments

Most of the material in this text is based on data drawn from actual classroom encounters, which we recorded and then transcribed to facilitate analysis. Changes and adaptations were necessary in some instances before inclusion in the text in order to highlight a particular point or dramatize a specific relationship. In presenting oral material in written form, we are forced to cut out one dimension, the more dynamic one: the dimension of sound. To effectively achieve the purposes of this book, the text would supplement video tapes of the encounters.

We are indebted to all the participants in these encounters. In addition, we extend thanks to: Russel Windes, our editor, for insight, guidance, and encouragement; John DeCecco, Joseph A. DeVito, and Margaret Linney for their advice on the manuscript; and to Nanine Bilski, Esther A. Bremer, Doris C. James, and Gerri Light for inestimable assistance.

Contents

PHASE 1

THE CLASSROOM
ENCOUNTER

*When I first get up in the morning I feel
fresh and it seems like it would be a good
day to me. But after I get in school,
things change and they seem to turn into
problems for me. And by the end of the
day I don't even feel like I'm young.
I feel tired.*

VICTOR Y., age 13

from *the me nobody knows*

The System

Like it or not, our classrooms today *must* be a microcosm of the world at large. For years we have paid lip service to this concept, represented by so-called progressive methodology—in classrooms from nursery to graduate school—while we have continued to stuff students with questionable material to be regurgitated on a Friday examination to give the teacher satisfaction or dismay depending upon the score "achieved." The popular educational philosophy "we learn by doing" has been misconstrued by teachers to mean that the instructors "do" while students observe the performances. But a world that moves from crisis to crisis requires human beings who have been trained to understand their position and responsibility in the communication process today. It is a matter of human survival. The classroom must be managed as a complex, ever-changing communication system composed of a multiple of *human variables;* and these human variables must determine how communication skills can be employed for the clearest, most appropriate communication in a given situation, in class or out.

Man has made enormous technological strides in our time, but whatever these advancements, human speech is still the ultimate tool. We depend on speaking and hearing for basic clarifications, for rapid and essential confirmation and clarification, even when the most sophisticated and precise technical devices are yielding more information than we really need. We wait for verification via the human voice. Consider the importance of human speech in the following words, taken from the

3

transcript of perhaps the most dramatic event ever shared by a world-wide communication system thus far in the twentieth century:

> EAGLE (the lunar module):   Houston, Tranquility Base here. The Eagle has landed.
> HOUSTON: Roger, Tranquility, we copy you on the ground. You've a bunch of guys about to turn blue. We're breathing again. Thanks a lot.
> EAGLE: Thank *you.*
> HOUSTON: You're looking good here.[1]

As the dialogue above indicates, only when the spoken words "Eagle has landed" were heard by "a bunch of guys about to turn blue," only when the verbal behavior confirmed the event being viewed by millions on television, did the experts in Houston, Texas, and the world at large start "breathing again." The *New York Times* headlines the next day told of a "voice from the moon," speaking to "an awed and excited audience of hundreds of millions of people on earth" and providing a statement that was repeated everywhere for days and continues to be quoted: "That's one small step for man, one giant leap for mankind."

Furthermore, when we consider the chances for survival on *this* planet—what have we planned for that ultimate moment when mankind may be on the brink of self-destruction, when the deadliest weapons are about to be launched for mass annihilation? Our last planned resort is a "hot line," a direct telephone line between two powers—two human beings, essentially—who must rely on communication to save mankind. Technology arranged this terrible interchange, just as technology carried man to the dusty craters of the moon. Only the skills of human speech and a controlled understanding of the communication process can save the world at that point.

The central issue here, then, is that virtually anything is possible in our world—including total annihilation; but our central source of control today, our remaining instrument for essential meaning in a critical situation is still the human communication system. Is it not, therefore, the teacher's responsibility to train students to participate knowingly and intelligently as a crucial element of a communication system?

The complexity of human communication has become the subject of study for scholars from many disciplines. The behavioral scientist records the results of man's communicative acts; the psychologist observes the individual communicating with his environment and interprets his behav-

---

[1] *The New York Times,* July 21, 1969, p. 1.

ior; the sociologist studies intergroup communication, the anthropologist intercultural behavior; the kinesiologist is concerned with certain aspects of nonverbal communication. All specialize in a portion of the total communication system, just as physicians and surgeons may specialize in a very limited part of the human organism. Only the general practitioner looks at the whole body, and the general practitioner in the study of communication is the teacher. Although the teacher may think of himself as a mathematician or a historian in the classroom, he is primarily involved in communication—his main task is the successful operation of a communication system.

HOW THE COMMUNICATION SYSTEM OPERATES

Here is how the communicative relationship operates in terminology used by systems theorists: The speaker provides an input by processing ideas into words and sound waves; the listener's sensory organs pick up the sound waves, which are then processed by being converted into words and ideas. The listener in turn responds with an output of behavior, which feeds back to the speaker information regarding the success of the original input and thus completes the simplest of communication systems.

The concepts essential to an understanding of systems theory are input, process, output, and feedback. Each of these terms can be illustrated in a much simpler system than that of communication. For example, consider the system that produces scrambled eggs (most people call such a system a recipe). According to the *All New Fannie Farmer Boston Cooking School Cookbook* the ingredients, or input, are eggs, salt, pepper, milk, and butter. The procedures for making scrambled eggs are to break the eggs into a bowl; add salt, pepper, and milk; mix the ingredients; heat the pan; melt the butter; and, finally, add the eggs. The processing continues with cooking over a low heat until creamy, stirring constantly, and scraping from the bottom and sides of the pan. After the processing is finished, the result obtained is a product of the ingredients but bears little resemblance to the raw materials. The feedback that confirms for the cook the success of the system is in the taste and in the texture of the eggs as they appear on the plate.

Now let us apply the same terms to the communication system. A speaker has a message with which he hopes to influence his environment. It must be encoded—put into words and formulated into vibrating particles of air. Just as eggs must be subjected to heat, the message must be changed into code form. And processing is important on the receiving end as well. The receiver must decode the message, or there is no output from the system: The eggs may be cooked, but unless someone eats them, the system is not complete. A message may be encoded, but the system is not complete until a receiver responds in some manner. The response may be internal rather than overt.

In solving a problem, the computer technician goes through similar steps. He feeds data into the computer along with the processing directions provided by a programmer. The computer processes or organizes the data into new relationships and produces a print-out of the results. There is little similarity between the print-out and the initial input, which was in most cases unrelated data. The processing has made data meaningful and useful. The teacher is part of a communication system in a classroom. He is a technician who arranges for the data of ideas to be fed into the system and processes the ideas into a mutually understood symbolic code. The ideas are subjected to the interaction of a group, and the output, or result of words, is a synthesis of what once was just data.

These illustrations of a system are intended to help you think of communication as more than a simple habitual act. Communication is an extremely complex form of human behavior in which the input consists of the speaker and all his motivations, the processing of coding and then decoding a message, and the output is the understanding of the message by the listener and the behavior, called "feedback," that tells the speaker how successful his system is.

The simplest communication system consists of two people. One person has a message. He encodes, puts his message into sound waves, which are detected by the ear of the listener. The listener decodes and responds in some fashion. By responding orally, the listener exchanges roles with the speaker, and the system continues. Such two-person communication systems are called *dyads*.

In the classroom the same process is going on with the listener-speaker roles clearly defined most of the time (see Figure 1–1):

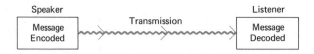

Fig. 1–1

In the classroom the teacher sends most of the messages, and the student spends most of his time as the listener rather than having equal time to speak, as he might in conversation. But Figure 1–1 does not provide a complete view of the system. Even though the student is listening, he is sending both verbal and nonverbal messages (feedback) back to the speaker. Facial expressions and posture, examples of nonverbal feedback, tell the speaker how the listener feels about the input of the system, even though the listener may not say a word. Figure 1–2 provides a more complete picture.

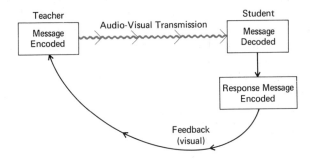

Fig. 1–2

FEEDBACK

The first characteristic of a communication system is that feedback is constantly used as input to control the operation of the system. Every observable response of an individual conveys some kind of message to those who are with him. Thus we say that man is always communicating, verbally or nonverbally. Every reaction we have to our environment, every attempt we make to change that setting tells those around us something about our own thoughts, feelings, and intentions. This feedback of reaction to the messages or stimuli around us determines, to some degree, the kinds of input others will provide for the system. These reactions and adaptations also tell us something about ourselves. In addition, we also get feedback from monitoring ourselves. We use this feedback in determining our subsequent messages or to modify messages already encoded. An example would be: "When I was five years old, I dreamed there was a peanuts . . . I mean a peanut. . . ." When the speaker, whose thinking preceded his speaking, hears the error in speech, his self-feedback immediately alerts him to the inaccuracy, and he returns to adjust the message.

Let us assume that a ten-year-old boy throws his ball into the air, and it sails over a fence and lands in the next yard. He sees a four-year-old child playing on the other side of the fence. His message (input) is, "I want my ball." He begins to process his input into polite code and says aloud, "Please throw the red ball back over the fence." He succeeds in drawing the child's attention to the ball. The latter processes the message and produces an output of response for the ten-year-old: He stands and stares at the older boy.

The ten-year-old does not get his desired feedback, the return of the ball, but he does receive some information. From the feedback he receives he can now predict that the four-year-old child is one of the following: hard of hearing, eager to keep the ball for himself, determined to demand some kind of payment for the service of throwing the ball over the fence, or hoping to be coaxed. The ten-year-old responds to his interpretations of the younger child's feedback with a new input and asks for the ball again. This time the small child shakes his head from side to side. This second negative feedback tells the older boy that the child is not hard of hearing and makes him suspect that, whatever the reason, the younger child is going to give him further difficulty. The owner of the ball has received an output, or print-out, by observation, but his system is not producing the results he wants.

Thus, feedback is a controlling factor in processing. If it is positive, the system continues to operate in a straight line, so to speak. If the feedback is negative, the succeeding input may be changed and may even go so far as to extinguish the whole system. The feedback of a communication system is extremely complex in that it affects not only the behavior of the sender of the message but also his perception of other messages. Feedback may affect our perceptions of ourselves and thus our attitudes. Consider the following dialogue between a ten-year-old girl and her mother:

> SUE: I don't like my teacher.
> MOTHER: Why?
> SUE: She made us all stay after school because the boys were noisy.
> MOTHER: But yesterday you said she was very nice because she taught you a new game in recess.
> SUE: I don't like that game very much.

Sue liked the game yesterday. But today its appeal has diminished because it is inconsistent with her judgments of her teacher. Now, challenged by the inconsistency of her judgments, Sue tries to adjust her first statement in order to justify her present feelings. Feedback has resulted in a change in the original sender of the message because her perception of the teacher has changed, and this has had a direct effect on the resulting message—" I don't like that game very much."

The phenomenon of feedback acting on a communication system is thus somewhat comparable to the operation of a self-adjusting camera in which a built-in light meter measures the amount of illumination in an environment and automatically adjusts the camera accordingly.

A NONLINEAR SYSTEM

The second characteristic of the communication system is that it is not linear in its operation. Although the diagrams you have seen imply that one event follows another, the communication system has many interacting processes going on at once. The human brain can in some ways be compared to a digital computer, which moves in single steps at a very rapid rate, but an even better analogy is with the analog computer, which deals with patterns rather than a binary language. The human brain scans and adjusts to several inputs at one time and controls several processes simultaneously and often unconsciously.

The complexity of the operation of the communication system may be illustrated by the following transcript from a third-year high school class studying American literature. Before this conversation took place, the class had been divided into small groups, which had prepared reports to be presented to the whole class. The small groups are now back in the large group to evaluate the reports. A girl has just finished a summary of her group's work on the symbolism in Ernest Hemingway's *A Farewell to Arms.*

Teacher: I want to hear from you first of all. What do you think of their interpretation of symbols? I hope you have something down. Do you have any questions? (*Addressing student from discussion group*) Why don't you call on them and answer their questions? And I'll just listen.

Carl (*sarcastically*):   Well, *some* of those things might be symbolic.

Teacher: Don't use that tone of voice.

Carl: Well, I mean some might be symbols, like the ants, maybe, but the rest of it. . . .

General discussion follows, with much overlapping.

Teacher: Wait a minute, Carl, will you? . . . Where does it say that?

Carl: You know, where the ants fall off the log into the fire. That's the only thing in the novel worth mentioning as a symbol, but the rest. . . . You're reading too much into it.

Student
Chairman: You want to pull symbolism out of the ants, right?

Another
Voice: O.K. That's about the end of that.

Student	
Chairman:	The question was, what symbolism is there in trees, and moun-tains, rivers, and lakes—that's the question. We answered it.
Carl:	And you said nothing.
Another	
Voice:	Oh, Carl!
Carl:	You found symbolism because that's what you were looking for. How much did Hemingway mean when he wrote the book?
Teacher:	Is that an issue?
Voice:	No.
Teacher:	Must we always take an author's intention in a book, or can we find our own meanings?

Carl's initial response is not a question, as specified by the directions, and the teacher feels his "tone of voice" might discourage comment; but such an immediate and strong "message" of feeling serves as a stimulus to interest and provokes reactions from others, who in turn adjust their own responses to what Carl is saying. At the point where Carl accuses the group of "reading too much into it," the class reacts to the verbal message as well as to his tone of voice or his vocal messages. These factors are interacting. Although the teacher's original processing directions are not being followed (and thus his program for the system is not working), the system is not a failure. Even though order in the discussion breaks down, the students are thinking about the message of the report on symbolism and about Carl's behavior. The class feedback changes Carl's attitude from sarcastic to assertive even though Carl's words indicate that he has not changed his mind about the book's symbolic content.

Communication consists of many simultaneous inputs, processes, and outputs. The fact that most of the time one idea tends to follow another in a classroom discussion makes us think that we are observing a simple linear system when actually it is very complex.

SUBSYSTEMS

The third characteristic of the communication system follows directly from its nonlinearity: Almost every system contains many simultaneously operating subsystems. The subsystem is analogous to the single kernel, one of hundreds of kernels of "popping" popcorn. All the corn receives heat from the larger source but each kernel "pops" independently. In addition, the single kernel functioning alone releases heat that affects the processing of the other kernels. When all these actions and effects are put together, we have the output of the larger system; when all the subsystems operating between students and students, student and student, teacher and student, and between the teacher and the students are put together, we have the system of the classroom. There is always a subsystem of communication between each individual student and the teacher in the classroom because of the teacher's special role in the group.

The next transcript illustrates the operation of a subsystem in a fifth-grade class in an inner-city school in Queens, a borough of New York City. Because a teachers' strike was in effect, a group of artists and musicians who were not part of the school teaching staff volunteered their services to provide classroom experiences for the students. The unorthodox teaching encounters proved to be exciting and profitable for the students. In this transcript the regular teacher (Mr. Horn) has returned to the classroom, where some musicians, and a video-taping team as well, are present. The teacher and the other adults immediately set up a subsystem in the classroom. Even the words Mr. Horn ostensibly directs to the class are in reality a reflection of the subsystem set up between him and the "outsiders." (In the teacher's monologue "Mr. Cannon" is a student, "Mr. Wilson" is a teacher's assistant, and "Mrs. Tosh" has custody of the audio-visual equipment. The teacher occasionally refers to himself as "Mr. Horn.")

Teacher: Sit down. Books away. If you want me to do my next lesson, I have a film strip projector and a film. All right, fine. Books away. If you want what I think is a fairly good lesson and really shows what's on these children's minds, Mr. Cannon, can you get Mr. Wilson to persuade Mrs. Tosh to bring in "New York City Is," right now at this moment? If he wants to go ahead and film what this class is capable of doing and what this class is capable of saying, let Mr. Wilson persuade Mrs. Tosh to give us "New York City Is." (*Turns to child who is talking to one of the "outsiders"*) Excuse me. You're talking to me?

Child: No.

Teacher: No? That's just it. You're speaking to *me* now. As far as you're concerned, we're the only ones here, regardless of what's going on over there. Now many weeks ago Mr. Horn brought up from downstairs this series of pictures for the bulletin board about "New York Is." And if you're looking at that, last week Mr. Horn got a book from the New York Urban League, and you cut out different pictures about what "New York Is." Excuse me. Can I continue? And if you'll look in the back, you'll see many different scenes of New York, of children playing in a project, of a father taking care of his daughter. What else is going on? Hands? Mr. Cannon. Come and point to the picture that you're talking about. O.K. Who else would like to come up and tell what exactly they see, what New York really is about. Deborah, please don't block the picture. What are those people

Child: doing in that picture? Well, why don't you go up and take a good close look?

Child: They're singing.

Teacher: What do you think they might be singing?

Child: Gospel songs.

Teacher: Gospel songs? What makes you think they're singing gospel songs? O.K. Thank you. All right. Let's have a discussion of another one of these four pictures, and I want to remind you these pictures are just one of the many pictures that we were discussing when we had the urban educational social studies lesson. Yes. What is going on? Making a speech? What about the other people in the picture? . . .

Child: They're singing.

Teacher: Again, what could they be singing? You saw gospels as Miss Jones pointed out. Anyone else? What could they be singing besides gospels? Mr. Brown.

Child: They could be praying.

Teacher: Praying? About what?

Child: About God and about heaven, and they pray about what's happening up there.

Teacher: (*turning to musicians and observers*): If you want to see this class really expose many different social issues, I suggest that any time you want you come into this class and I will do my urban education lesson. And you'll see some of the most creative minds at work. And many children in this class, although they may be in a lower exponent class [*sic*], have a tremendous amount of creativity. It's there to be gotten out of them, and any time you want to come in you're more than welcome. And these children will open up their hearts to you and me and to the world.

In this exchange the interaction between the students and the teacher is secondary to the interaction between the teacher and the "outsiders." The teacher is using the messages addressed to the class as a means of expressing his hostility to the "outsiders" who threaten him. This attitude is perhaps best illustrated when Mr. Horn says to the onlookers, ". . . I suggest that any time you want you come into this class and I will do my urban education lesson."

SYMMETRICAL AND COMPLIMENTARY RELATIONSHIPS

The subsystem of relationships between student and teacher are as important as the content of the message—and sometimes overpower the message. The relationships may be designated as either symmetrical or complementary. In the earlier example, when the younger child did not return the ball, he may have felt himself equal to the older boy; the relationship was therefore symmetrical. If the child had returned the ball without question, the relationship would have been complementary; that is, one person would have been in the "up" position and the other in the "down" position. Neither position or relationship is less desirable than the other unless it is inappropriate to the situation or degrading to the one in the "down" position. For the most part, these relationships between individuals are only temporary and are readjusted according to the feedback each individual is picking up. In the family constellation the parent-child relationship is usually complementary, with the parent being in the "up" position. The teacher's relationship with a student also tends to be complementary since, traditionally, the teacher is an authority figure who initiates, leads, and summarizes "learning." The teacher also makes regular evaluative judgments: grades. Therefore, the traditional student-teacher relationship is more complementary than most other nonfamily personal associations.

The teacher in the inner-city school seemed to be trying to be "in command" of his class and to hold the "up" position. He obviously felt threatened by the other adults in the room (the television cameramen) and used the children as vehicles for attaining more stature. By contrast, the teacher of the American literature class willingly relinquished his position to a student leader, moving freely from the complementary to the symmetrical role in order to facilitate discussion and participation.

THE CLASSROOM—AN EXPERIMENT IN COMMUNICATION

An understanding of the theory of communication does not guarantee proficiency in communicating but is the first step in making the teacher a "communication technician" for the classroom. For most teachers undertaking such a communication experience will seem to illustrate the high odds that exist against success in even the simplest of communications, since few human beings are trained to control and analyze the communication system. In the classroom, at least, the student needs to learn to control his spoken verbal code with a precision that contributes meaningfully to reasonable accuracy in communicative systems.

By employing literal classroom transcripts in these chapters, we are able to record with some accuracy the actual words a student used. But the sounds of the tape-recorded language are lost to the reader of the transcript. Indeed, unless written language is carefully marked with symbols (such as phonetics and intonation patterns), a speculative realm of meaning is always present. The author of the printed material is usually not present for amplification of the printed word. But in the transcripts the reader can determine where the communication process might have been interrupted and where the teacher might have led the student to discover the basis for confusion. The transcripts represent a traditional structure of teaching and learning within the classroom; the teacher feeds a student previously ordered data; the students return that data or an amplification or modification of that data at some future time in another form: a test, an oral report, a term paper. Learning is ordinarily measured by the evaluation of such a subsequent "product." Yet even in these traditional classroom activities the central concern must always be in the understanding and evaluation of the communication design. What is the system? What are the subsystems? Is the processing controlled through intelligent manipulation of the communicator's verbal code? Is the listening at a responsible level? What is the nature of the feedback? What are the emotional and intellectual elements in the content of the communication system? Ideally, the classroom would be the laboratory in which human beings would be developing communication skills for solving problems and making decisions that arise and develop within that laboratory.

In the following transcript of an eighth grade let us assume that the behavior described arose from a class that was attempting to understand its responsibility as a communication system, a class from which arose the necessity of organizing a mock Presidential election to clarify an aspect of the American governmental process for an assembly. The transcript comprises a rehearsal of one eighth grader's "speech" to the "convention" regarding Richard Nixon's qualifications as a Presidential candidate; other students and the teacher from Jay's communication laboratory— Jay's classroom—assist:

Jay: Richard Milhous Nixon was born January 9, 1913, in California. Married Patrick Ryan and has three daughters, Patricia, 22, and Julie, 19. His past positions he held are Vice-President of the United States from 1953 to 1961. He was senator from 1951 to 1952. He was a United States Naval officer in World War II and was an attorney of law before he became a senator. As Vice-President he settled the steel strike that would've upset the whole economy of this nation. He also debated Khrushchev at the American exhibition in Moscow. He was the highest-ranking American to visit the U.S.S.R. He received the greatest welcome of any Westerner ever to visit Poland. He also won great praise for his statesmanlike handling of crises in three Presidential illnesses. While he was in Congress, he won a seat in the Senate by 700,000 votes. He was also endorsed in 1948 by Democrats and Republicans for reelection. In 1968 he helped

get the 1968 Civil Rights Bill out of the committee and on the
House floor for vote.

Fellow
Student: Jay, I'm pretending I am a sixth grader. What does "endorse"
mean? Could you tell that to a sixth-grade class? Would they
be able to figure what it meant?

Jay: "Endorse" means. . . .

Student: I know what it means, but would they? And his wife's name
is Patrick?

Jay: Patricia.

Student: Be careful of that.

Teacher: Do we have another question, now, please?

Another
Student: What was the third daughter's name?

Jay: Two daughters.

Student: You said there were three.

Jay: I've got—I wrote down three. Then I crossed it out, and I put
down two.

Again, if we assume that the situation above emerged as an experiment
by a group beginning to probe the responsibilities of human communication, the student questions were reasonable, if somewhat vague and
random. Jay's fellow students questioned his responsibility as an encoder
making conscious verbal code choices ("endorse") for a *known* group of
decoders; his concentration and control of meaning through accurate
pronunciation ("Patrick" for "Patricia"); his consistency and logical presentation of factual, denotative information (he mentioned "three
daughters" and named two). Although Jay's fellow communicators
seemed concerned in helping Jay clarify his communication, questions
such as the following might have provided a better basis for evaluation of
Jay's attempted communication:

Are your words selected for easy comprehension and minimal connotative
possibility?

Are the facts accurate?

Are your facts arranged in logical order to maintain an unbiased, re-
portorial point of view?

Does your use of your native language reflect your concern for grammatical clarity and correctness as a responsible communicator in this kind of
communication system (one encoder processing a communication to many
relatively silent encoders whose feedback is, in general, limited to gesture
and movement)?

Are you controlling the actual process of encoding at whatever conscious level necessary for accurate processing?

If your aim is to be a reporter, is your voice in delivery communicating the *attitude* of a reporter?

Are you familiar enough with your material in this form of communication system to adjust your communication to any feedback—positive or negative —that you may encounter?

These are a few of the possible questions that fellow students might pose, that Jay himself might consider before participating in this formalized, prepared communication system.

The classroom, then, must become a communication laboratory in a modern world; a human relations laboratory in which the human variable—the student—strives to understand and develop his role in every aspect of modern communication. He must exercise as encoder, processor, and decoder the emotional and intellectual content of a message. Whether in kindergarten, eighth grade, or college, whether participating in a group communication system, an intimate dyad, or the various possible communication system arrangements, the verbal communicator must work for conscious and conscientious meaningful control of the communication system in which he is participating.

Martin Duberman in "An Experiment in Education," an essay reflecting his experiences with a particular class at Princeton University, summarizes our challenge this way:

> Competition continues to be the hallmark of our society because we continue to train our youth to act competitively, to measure their worth in terms of how successfully they dominate others rather than themselves.
>
> The grading system also trains young Americans to be more adept at judging others than at understanding them, and at judging, moreover, on the basis of limited and largely unattractive qualities: how well an individual "performs" in public; how readily he assimilates established values; how responsive he is to pressure situations; how adept he is at memorizing and verbalizing; how mechanically he can provide right answers; how obediently he can avoid "wrong" questions.
>
> I do not doubt that tests and grades prepare the student for the American life style. The question is whether we approve of that style and wish to perpetuate it.[2]

[2] Martin Duberman, *The Uncompleted Past* (New York: Random House, 1969), pp. 284–285.

Two

The Setting

In the first chapter we discussed classrooms as systems and subsystems. This relabeling provides a new way of looking at old interactional patterns. Good teaching will always be good teaching. And bad teaching, unfortunately, will always be bad teaching whether it is described in systemic terms or not. But by looking at the classroom from another point of view, perhaps fresh insights will be discovered and relationships dramatized.

Systems theory is a technique for analyzing problems by providing a framework in which multiple inputs producing specific outputs can be isolated, examined, and evaluated. In some cases these outputs are predetermined (scrambled eggs), but in others they are subject to variation, as is usually the case in human interaction (a class). Monumental scientific and technological tasks have been accomplished by means of systems. The success of the systems theorists working in the United States space program has encouraged the application of similar techniques to analyze and confront social problems.

How can systems theory be used to describe and codify communication encounters in the classroom so as to specify more clearly what is involved in the communicative act? How can the teacher generate situations in which students can experiment with their communication skills? How can the teacher act as the facilitator of a system rather than as a linear programmer?

THE CONCEPT OF INTERACTION

The communication system in a classroom is made up of "small" interactions among two or more members of the class. Each interaction constitutes a subsystem influencing the functioning of the total system of the class. The systems approach improves upon the cause-and-effect or stimulus-response theories in two ways: by taking into account the many kinds of input that exist in classrooms; by making the actual processing of the inputs a separate and definable element. Students by their verbal and nonverbal behavior are constantly communicating their reactions to each other and to the teacher, thus affecting and shaping the classroom encounter. Systems theory substitutes this concept of interaction for the concept that views the teacher's participation as a kind of performance with limited feedback possibilities between him and his "audience." Output can be isolated as a result of the input and processing and can be compared with the outputs of similar systems so that meaningful judgments of change and progress can be made. By using the systems concept as a metaphor for the classroom encounter, the teacher himself can see clearly the several interrelated elements of input, such as verbal language, nonverbal language, and perceptual patterns. Finally, the importance of feedback is clarified, and failures or breakdowns in the system can be located and identified.

The classroom is the inevitable field of encounter for the learning experience, but the result of that experience can be greatly influenced by the way the teacher views classroom interaction. Systems theory provides a means of codifying the classroom interaction and allows the teacher to examine particular segments of this interaction independently as well as in relation to the whole. By this means the teacher can place the emphasis where it is most appropriate for the student; that is, on the processing, for in our present culture it is more important for the student to know how to process a message than to store it. The informational content of our lives changes and widens so rapidly that the need for techniques of organization and analysis of that information supersedes memorization as the most important item for storage.

THE CLASSROOM—A TEMPORARY SYSTEM

Considered as a system, the classroom derives certain advantages from the fact that it is a temporary and not a permanent system. Matthew Miles, in his essay on "Temporary Systems," distinguishes between temporary and permanent systems by stating that "members [of temporary systems] hold from the start the basic assumption that—at some more or less clearly defined point in time—they will cease to be." In Miles' view the temporary system possesses these advantages:

> For one thing, since communication to groups outside is far less than that within the system, a common language with special meanings for the participants tends to grow up. Secondly, new channels of information transmission tend to develop between persons whose roles in former permanent systems have kept them apart. Thirdly, since increased interaction leads to increased liking, other things being equal, there is a strong tendency for participants to share more information with each other, become more open and trustful. Finally, under these conditions, equal status relationships develop among participants, so that persons are not seen as having the right to withhold or distort information, as is ordinarily the case [for good reasons] in permanent structures. [Miles' brackets][1]

The conditions Miles sets in defining a temporary system are all inherent in the nature of the classroom: a relatively stable membership; a predetermined goal that can be changed in light of new information generated by the group; and a predetermined sentence of "death," a date of dissolution.

THE ROLE OF THE TEACHER AS FACILITATOR

For the classroom encounter the most important of Miles' conditions is that which has a particular cogency for the role of the teacher in today's classroom: The teacher is viewed as a "facilitator" who uses his skills when they are needed to assist the group. Psychotherapist Carl Rogers, who applies analytic theories to educational practice, has argued in favor of a "facilitator" concept of the teacher's role. In his book *Client-Centered Therapy* he discusses this kind of student-centered teaching. The teacher, as facilitator, gives information and directs the discussion as needed, but he does not establish himself as the sole leader of the group. Evaluations of classes that function in such a nondirective way indicate that "most students tend to work harder and at a deeper level, than in the conventional course."[2] The students sense a greater relevancy of the subject matter to their own lives and gain a greater understanding of themselves.

[1] Matthew Miles, *Innovation in Education* (New York: Teachers College Press, 1964), p. 467.
[2] Carl R. Rogers, *Client-Centered Therapy* (Boston: Houghton Mifflin, 1951), p. 419.

The following transcript is a classroom discussion, in an inner-city junior high school, of a reading selection about the Irish famine of 1846. The teacher is the director of the linear system rather than the facilitator of a group using the system to meet their own needs. Notice that each comment made by a child must receive feedback from the teacher, who then adds input to evoke another response from the child. The children are learning little about controlling or evaluating their own communication. The teacher tells the students what he wants as an answer rather than helping them to assess the appropriateness of their own ideas.

Teacher: I'm trying to find out what mood is being described in each paragraph. First of all what do we mean by mood? What do you understand by mood? What does it mean? What is mood to you?

Child: A feeling.

Teacher: All right. What feeling do you get after reading that passage?

Child: You feel good, and you're nice to everybody.

Teacher: All right. What does mood mean besides feeling? Can you give us another adjective?

Child: Reactions.

Teacher: All right. Your reaction.

Child: It could be how you feel about things. Expression.

Teacher: Your expression. All right. (Teacher assigns student to read paragraph from text.) What mood did you have when you heard the reading? What do you see? What images do you see?

Child: I see frightening and evil.

Teacher: What do you see?

Child (*with a gloomy attitude*): Because they're thinking about the evil things done, so they feel gloomy when they think about it.

Teacher: All right. Anybody else see another mood in these two paragraphs?

Child: A mood of the last light.

Teacher: All right. The last light. Anything else? I see some clue words in there. Evil spirits. What does that bring to mind?

Child: Superstition.

Teacher: Superstition. All right. Anything else? Any other moods? What mood does superstition bring to you?

Child: Fear.

Teacher: Fear and what else?

Child: Worry.

Teacher: Worry? Why does it make you think of worry?

Child: 'Cause the evil spirits are goin' to scare you.

Teacher: The evil spirits might scare them. How could they scare them?

Child: They could chase them away.

Teacher: How would this affect the farmers?

Child: It would take away their crops.
Teacher: And what was their crop?
Child: Potatoes.
Teacher: Potatoes. And was this a very important crop? For this area?
Child: Yes.
Teacher: What area was this? Do you remember? What's the setting of the story?
Child: Ireland.
Teacher: Ireland. Right before what happened?
Child: Immigration to America.
Teacher: Immigration to America because of what reasons?
Child: Because the people left Ireland and came to America to see the country.
Teacher: But why did they leave? Did they have to leave?
Child: Because they were too poor to live in the country.
Child: They didn't have enough work in Ireland so they moved to America.
Teacher: What type of work did they do? What type of work?
Child: Potato growing?
Teacher: They grew potatoes. And what happened that now they didn't have any work to do? What happened?
Child: The potatoes got destroyed.
Teacher: The potatoes were destroyed by what? Do you remember?
Child: By the potato blight.

The teacher's intention in this communication system is to produce an understanding of mood (itself a vague concept). But achieving this output is something more than simply prodding students to find synonyms for the word. An understanding of any mood requires some sensory memory and the ability to verbalize a sensory experience. The teacher might have considered the kinds of sensory images her students had. This would mean that she had examined the input into the system and should have realized that a group of junior high school students, most of whom are black and enrolled in a public school system in the inner city, could never have any sensory understanding of the effect of the potato famine on Irish farmers in Ireland more than a century ago. Instead, she might have considered the possible experiences of the young people in this classroom and start with these as the input; through adept processing she might have led the class, by means of their own additions to the system, to some comprehension of mood. Furthermore, here the teacher is strictly controlling the processing so that it must proceed linearly. She consistently asks questions that are self-limiting—that is, her questions require a single answer, and there is little room for the student to interpolate or bring his own ideas into the discussion. The teacher further controls the system by being the evaluator of the responses and not allowing the student to serve as critic either for himself or for his peers. As a result, a discussion that began by investigating the abstract concept of mood ends with the informational storage of facts regarding the potato blight. Compare the input of this actual system with the suggested input of a hypothetical system. In the hypothetical system the input is designed to let the children control the system by asking their own questions and freely contributing their own ideas rather than passively allowing the teacher to guide them to present "acceptable" replies. The teacher seldom overtly evaluates the class' input into the system but facilitates a self-evaluation by the class itself by stimulating the students' imagination and providing subsystems to engender discussion and ideas.

Teacher: I'm going to say some words that we heard in these paragraphs. I want you to jot down what feeling they give you. "Chilly wind," "dark night," "squeaky door," "misty cloud."

(*Children follow directions and are given sufficient time for a series of answers.*)

Teacher: Let's read our reactions.

(*Students read their jottings.*)

Teacher: There were lots of answers. Which ones did you feel were most accurate, and *why*?

(*Discussion by members of the class*)

Teacher: Did some who just talked tell us how they feel by the way they said the words?

(*More class discussion*)

Teacher: You heard a reading of the story by a student, with his way of saying the feeling. Now divide into small groups for ten minutes and decide if there is another possible feeling for these words. Choose a member of your group to read the story for us to illustrate the feeling your group has decided upon. We will try to determine what you found.

(*Later, after a reading*)

Teacher: We've agreed that Jane read the passage appropriately with an attitude, a feeling, of worry. Return to your groups for five minutes and see if you can figure out why evil spirits could make these people worry.

(*After five minutes children offer explanations of how evil spirits create worry.*)

Teacher: Tell us about an experience *you* have had that created feelings in you that were similar to those of the people in the story.

(*Students respond.*)

Teacher: Is there anything in the story which helps us understand the attitudes of the Irish people during the potato famine?

(*Students respond.*)

Teacher: Let's evaluate our discussion. How did the sharing of our own
experience help us to gain insight into the problems of others?
(*Students respond.*)

The second system attempts to demonstrate how the teacher might
have drawn responses from the group's own experience and then elabo-
rated upon these. The second approach also allows for the student to
evaluate responses and select that which is most meaningful for him.

THE COMMUNICATION-ORIENTED CLASSROOM

The relevant output of the classroom today, more than ever before, is the
student's ability to relate to, and operate efficiently in, other communication systems. The student of the seventies, perhaps far better equipped
with vitality, commitment, and sophistication than students of other
decades, is critical of the breakdown of communication in society and
views it as one of the sources of the widespread dissatisfaction with the
status quo. The classroom provides a laboratory for the development and
practice of communication skills: All of the problems of human communication can occur in the classroom, yet the participants are relieved of
the necessity of suffering the consequences of their failures. Instead they
may contemplate the consequences and learn from them. Learning that
takes place in the classroom inevitably occurs within a communication
system of some kind; thus, even within such structured subject matter as
mathematics, the student solves problems and works at the same time on
his communicative relationships with peers and authority figures.

The classroom is first of all a communication system and secondly a
learning situation. It can be a system that operates by trial and error,
sometimes successfully and sometimes not. Or, in the communication-
oriented class, both students and teacher can become aware of the
elements of input and processing and can learn increasingly to monitor
their output and thus deliberately control the functioning of the system.

In time the student will be able to:

1. Produce unique communications with emotional and intellectual content in an environment that is not threatening and that allows for free
   interchange of ideas among peers and teacher
2. Play the role of the "second speaker" or the receiver of messages who
   listens willingly and responds with feedback that has meaningful
   intellectual and emotional content
3. Monitor his own communicative behavior and that of other speakers
   for analysis and evaluation

4. Control and improve his own communication and the operation of communication systems of which he is a part
5. Use his communication skills for solving problems and making decisions.

In subsequent chapters various processing techniques that give practice and aid in reaching these objectives will be explored. But before doing this, let us examine the internal sources of input that exist in all groups and affect the functioning of communication systems.

INTERNAL SOURCES OF INPUT

The teacher who views his class as a temporary system or a small problem-solving group can take advantage of the properties inherent in all groups and use "group culture" to advance the common purpose. National Training Laboratories (NTL), an organization that has set up training groups (T-groups) in participation and leadership in group communication for both industrial and educational institutions, utilizes temporary systems or T-groups to achieve its objectives and focuses on bringing about changes in the individual participant.[3] These objectives are:

1. Increased awareness and sensitivity to his own emotional reactions and those of his companions
2. Greater ability to perceive and use feedback
3. Clarification and development of personal values and goals
4. Theoretical knowledge of group dynamics
5. Ability to perform more efficiently with small groups of people.

Each of these objectives relies on group interaction and the individual's learning from observing the other group members. The goals set by NTL are similar to the goals of a communication-oriented classroom; most T-groups, however, are set up for short and intensive training periods, whereas the classroom teacher usually has the advantage of more time in which to sharpen communication skills.

Two levels of interaction, internal and external, exist within all groups. These levels are distinct and at the same time related to each other, and together they account for the individuality of each group or the "group culture." They are distinct in that external interaction is the group's behavior in relation to its environment and tasks, and internal interaction is the sum of intragroup attitudes or feelings and the internalized behav-

[3] National Training Laboratories, *Towards the Improvement of Campus Life*, NTL, 1963.

ior of the group's individual members. The external behavior of a group reflects the group's internal relationships, of course, and successful functioning in the environment is related to the group's internal relationships. Obviously, congenial internal relationships among group members will make the problem-solving task easier and more pleasant.

Norms, or patterns of behavior expected of group members by other group members, emerge from the internal relationships of groups. An example of a norm is the expectation in most classrooms that students will raise their hands to be acknowledged by the teacher before speaking. This norm is so much a part of classroom behavior that when students find themselves in a class that does not adhere to the hand-raising ritual, they do not know how to participate. Not until some kind of internal relationship between class members is established and the new norm is allowed to develop does a productive informal discussion take place. The internal structure produces the group norms and is extremely important to the efficiency of the group in terms of the group's ability to deal with problems, make decisions, and complete tasks.

A class or group in which there are strong subsystems whose outputs conflict with the output of the total group system will not be as effective as the group in which the subsystems support the major purposes. The teacher who establishes smaller groups within the class and has them compete with each other will later find it difficult to have the class function as a whole without some of the competitiveness influencing the processing. "Winning" or "losing" should never be a goal in small-group activity. A teacher who is aware of the internal culture of the group takes this culture into account in making plans for the group's learning tasks, and he will probably be more successful in attaining his goals. Even the simple recognition of the existence of an internal culture can be a factor in influencing the successes and failures of various groups.

Once norms are developed, the communication system can be focused on external relationships. The group can seek to understand the poetry that they read or the differences between the qualifications of political candidates; they can explore the hypotheses for explaining a scientific phenomenon or seek a solution to student-administration conflict. When a class first meets, its members spend much time in the beginning in adapting to each other and simply getting to know the roles of each participant in the communcation system. Sociologist George Homans suggests that the kind and intensity of the internal relationships will determine the efficiency in handling the external relationships.[4] Some classes find all

[4] George C. Homans, *The Human Group* (New York: Harcourt Brace Jovanovich, 1950).

external tasks challenging because the members like to work with each other, while others struggle with boredom and inefficiency because the internal structure is not sufficiently developed.

HOW GROUP CULTURE OPERATES

To illustrate the functioning of "group culture," consider the interaction of a small group of college students discussing the meaning of the expression "black power." The group consists of two white males, Peter and Mike; two white females, Alice and Sylvia; and one black female, Gerri. Although the small group or communication net was drawn from a larger class in which relationships had begun to form, this was the first time that this particular group had met, and thus a new system was being shaped. Some adaptive behavior had to take place before the group could begin to function in relation to its task. Ideally, in the course of adaptation, a feeling of trust begins to develop through the removal of threats to individual participants. In this group the person who might be most justified in feeling threatened is Gerri, the black student, since she is in the minority. She expresses her fears in a statement early in the interaction:

> They came to me and said, "How about writing a column for the college newspaper?" I said, "Yeah, maybe!" Because I've had bad experiences with that paper. I decided that all news media is raunchy, because no matter what you say or write, it will always be misinterpreted, unless you get an opportunity like this to explain yourself. Speaking directly to a person about a topic can get you out of a lot of trouble. I can see myself—what I've written—dragged into the FBI. And when I'm trying to get a job in the future, being psyched just because of what I've written.

This student cannot trust the students who might read what she would write in the paper, but in the oral situation, with continuous feedback, she has adapted to the point of revealing ideas. She can adapt to what is happening. Later in the period Gerri says:

> But I'm trying to explain to you how many black people feel. I really can't lay the groundwork of how they become antagonized because it hasn't happened to me much at all. It only happened to me when I came to this school, the first year. It's very subtle. For me to explain to you—you probably wouldn't understand.

Even having the security of feedback for her ideas does not give this student the feeling that this group of white students can get her message. In another place she says, "I can't convince a white man." The black student must trust this particular group of white students enough to reveal feelings. At the same time the group must provide an environment of trust in which any student feels he can express his opinion without fear of attack. The means of establishing this environment is in a semisocial network. The group members must spend enough time together in a nonthreatening situation to know each other. Then they will have some basis for forming new membership patterns.

Further on in the discussion the following took place:

Alice: I'm so confused. We've strayed so far from the beginning. Like we started out to define "black power," and you've gotten into police brutality. Like we still haven't moved from where we were in the beginning.

Sylvia: I think we need a list of specific questions on each topic.

Alice: That's what happens each time. I keep asking for questions.

Sylvia: Let's get back to one point.

Alice: Like Gerri. She's answering everything. We're not answering anything. Like you know. What do you think?

Sylvia: I think Gerri has taken a lot of leadership.

Gerri: We're going to just sit here otherwise. Nobody's saying—what I was really trying to do was say some things that a few of you who have some great ideas would pick up and keep the conversation rolling. I'm sitting here, and I'm dying when nobody says anything.

At this point Alice and Sylvia have become actively aware of the difficulty of the group in making a communication system work toward its purpose. Sylvia, in particular, is beginning to emerge as the procedural leader; she is the person in the group who assumes the responsibility for keeping the group discussion channeled by providing suggestions to facilitate the processing of the communication system. Alice is also concerned with the processing of the group, but, as revealed later in the discussion, she is more concerned with the development of congenial relationships among the participants and making sure that everyone contributes to the discussion. The role that she is assuming is that of the socio-emotional leader. Gerri's special position in the group is demonstrated in the following interaction:

Peter: The average American does have a connotation of "black power" meaning: Burn America down. Well, look what happened in the riots last year. When H. Rap Brown can get up and say: "We're going to get out guns—we're going to shoot everybody in sight."

Gerri: I've seen H. Rap Brown. I've heard him talk. He couldn't start a riot if he had to. If it was a matter of life and death, he couldn't.

Mike: What are you saying? He doesn't hold a position of leadership?
Gerri: He has no charisma.

The student has not seen or heard Brown but is reporting information he gained from the media.

Without denying the statement, Gerri has discounted the importance of the claim and reduced the impact of the illustration of "black power." The group accepts her word, for she is the only black and maintains a special position in the group. She has been active in campus and black movements. Her words are accepted as having far more weight than anything presented by the media.

Alice: I want to get back to a point you said before—about the news media—and that they've built up the new connotation of "black power." True, the newspaper, TV, and any kind of press has the influence to stretch a point. I agree with that. But if they're reporting on something an individual says, and if he says we have to destroy to get our way, the media is not stretching any points there. He's just reporting.

Notice the attitude of this comment. The speaker is careful to initiate her comments by agreeing with Gerri and to phrase her personal views tentatively. Alice is establishing herself as socio-emotional leader.

Gerri has been claiming that the white students have gotten their concept of the term "black power" from the media but that black people have a different concept. Alice finds that the ideas from two authoritative sources conflict. She is accustomed to accepting the mass media as an accurate source of information. Yet now she hears an equally strong source telling her something quite different. What advantage does the small group have in this situation for reconciling the views, for determining the more accurate view?

First, the group provides a wider variety of backgrounds for judging the two sources than the individual's experience. Even if one of the sources were not present, the group would have a better base for evaluation than one person's opinion. It is likely that other possible solutions or explanations of the difference will be offered. The students are made aware of a situation in which there is not a single right answer. The group depends on the participants' attitudes toward maintaining an open acceptance of new ideas. There are negative aspects as well, because in the small group there is very little resistance to persuasive efforts by a strong leader.

Gerri: It's amazing the way things are presented by the media.
Sylvia: The intonation and the words have to be there for commentators to report it.

Gerri: I'm not saying they did this. You can take what I've said or what you say and switch it around to mean different things.

Sylvia: What I'm saying is that it takes two to write an article.

Gerri: I've seen H. Rap Brown. I saw him at City College. You know, he comes in and he's tall and he's fine looking and everyone's expecting him anyway. I mean you know where he's at. And he only wanted to speak to black people. We had been waiting like all month for this to happen. So he came down, and it was a great thing 'cause all your friends were there, people you hadn't seen for years. And he gets up and he talks, and he will do like that with his head. Now that was photographed, like I've seen him on Channel Two coming down an aisle going like this, you know. It really seems all wild. Goodness, that man is so wild. But he might be just doing it. When you're in the full context of the thing, it doesn't have that much of an impact. It doesn't even radiate that much feeling at all.

Alice: I understand your point, but when someone says "to get what we want we have to destroy the structure of the U.S.," that's not taking anything out of context.

Gerri: To some people that would mean destroy vice and corruption in government and make a clean democracy.

Notice that, in spite of a conscious analysis by the group, one student is the center of the thinking; the pattern is still evident.

Group communication systems constantly readjust to the needs of the members. There is only one divergent opinion from the acceptance of the mass media. The whole group is attempting to bring the one member into a pattern of agreement. This may mean that the large group will move to the position of the single divergent position. However, it also means that the divergent person will be the center of the group. Sometimes an individual deliberately takes an opposite point of view to stimulate discussion or to gain focus. However, this is usually detected by the members of the group who resent the manipulation of the process.

Alice: But there are so many ways of saying things without riling people to begin with.

Gerri: How many people use them?

Sylvia: I think if you put things in a different way, you might get a fairer response.

Peter: Destroying the structure of the U.S. does not mean to remedy or reform the vices. It means to destroy the structure.

Gerri: Are you the person who said it?

Peter: Well, this is the way—

Gerri: How do you know?

The white students are not so distant from the black student that they are afraid to disagree with her. They would very much like to believe that "black power" was not aimed at the destruction of white society, but they keep pressing for more evidence.

Gerri: See, that's why I refuse to write for the newspaper. Because any-
         thing I say with my background might come out completely differ-
         ent. I was quoted by the paper for saying something. I didn't mean
         to say it in the context. The fellow had even taken a term that I
         used and expanded it. So he didn't quote me. And people would
         come to me and ask, "How could you say that?" They were indig-
         nant.

Peter: Well, then Stokely Carmichael meant he wanted to remedy the
         vices. If that's what he meant when he said he wanted to destroy
         the structure of the U.S., I would say that he doesn't know much
         of the English language or he doesn't know what he's saying or
         he's just trying to goad people on because why did he say it that
         way? Why didn't he say he wanted to remedy the vices?

Gerri: I have not grown up with either H. Rap Brown or Stokely Car-
         michael. For example, Stokely Carmichael is from Trinidad. And
         West Indians by nature (and I'm making a generalization, and I'm
         making it because my parents are West Indians, so I know) are
         volatile, expressive people. They, well, like my father. Something
         cool happens to me and he will take it and it will mean the most
         impossible thing to him. It will upset him to the utmost. And this
         is the way from what I know this group of people are. Also you
         have another thing with Stokely Carmichael. Being he is West
         Indian, he has a fantastic amount of pride. Black men in the West
         Indies are the epitome of everything. They are worshiped. There
         isn't a single black man who hasn't had his ego built since he was
         an infant in the West Indies. And when they come to this garbage.
         First of all they won't accept it; they won't believe it. You think
         they are going to come here and see this garbage continue? They
         don't understand this sort of thing. And you expect Stokely Car-
         michael to just sit back and see people—in Trinidad everybody
         has black skin, even the East Indians and the Orientals— Isn't
         it foolish for him to be rejected only because of his skin?

Mike (*trying to interrupt*):   Well—

Gerri: And don't tell me he hasn't had the back of many hands!

The black student is speaking totally from her own experience and observation. Another black student might have an entirely different point of view. Peter is not ready to accept her assumption of that context or agree that the situation can make that much difference. He assumes the responsibility of challenging Gerri's statements.

At this point in the discussion the communication system is beginning to break down, and the cohesion that had been developed within the group is threatened. The task—to define "black power"—is not yet completed, but it can still be realized if Alice steps in as socio-emotional leader and works to develop group rapport and cohesion again and if Sylvia, as procedural and task leader, suggests directional questions that will bring the group back to its task.

That "black power" receives a definition is not essential to the purpose of the reader. What is important is that the reader is able to separate the external goals of the group from the internal structure of the group and observe that these college students were allowed to control their own communication network and deal with its inherent problems: of adapting to each other; developing leadership roles within the group, as needed; participating in an open and free discussion about an emotionally charged topic; and relating to each other in order to gain insights about their own and others' communicative behavior. This kind of analysis puts the stress on the processing of data rather than on the accumulation of data leading to the fixing of conclusions that might have to be changed at a later date.

This kind of analysis could not take place without the separation of input variables from the processing, and the processing from the output. The classroom teacher, as facilitator in a communication system, must recognize the input, control the processing, and identify the output of the system so that the student will have a sense of learning fulfillment.

PHASE 2

THE INPUT:
Experiencing Language in the Classroom

For what purpose was I born?
I don't see.
To speak words that no one will listen to
No matter how loud I shout them?
To throw up dates, and events just as
I recorded them and be pronounced a genius?
To sit through school day after day and
be referred to as a "good child"?
To hear things that I shouldn't
and then be instructed to forget? . . .

v.b., age 14

from *the me nobody knows*

Three

Verbal Behavior

The world is a teaching machine, and we internalize learning. Communicators universally use words, sounds, and gestures to represent literal components of their lives in their individual worlds. These abstractions and their various forms are organized for meaning by applying an established code—grammar—and the result is what we call language. For example, the sentence "The child crawls like a dog" carries meaning in English, since the words—written or spoken—are abstractions for literal elements in our lives that we readily recognize (except for the functional items "the," "like," and "a"); and the code, or word order, indicates who is doing what. In the sentence "The dog crawls like a child" the same abstractions—the words—signal different meaning because the code—the grammar of English—orders the abstractions differently. Furthermore, a particular language (English, French, Spanish, and so forth) may be considered to be the total of all the possible "sentences" that its "rules" of grammar allow; these "possibilities" in English for example are infinite. When we encode, process, and decode a message, we are using a minute portion of the possibilities that our grammar provides.

CODE SYMBOLS

Language, then, is the totality of our experiences internalized. If we understand the order needed to externalize the abstractions of our experiences, we may be said to be *competent* in our language, native or not.

The actual externalization into sound is language communication through speech. Speech employs the abstractions of words and gestures to symbolize aspects of the larger concept, language. Performance in speaking demonstrates competence.

The extent to which we take for granted the use of seeing and hearing for communication is not often realized. We do, of course, use our other senses as well in communicating. Touch as a means of conveying messages is used by both man and animals; odors are used more frequently by animals. Almost all of the sensory-motor mechanisms can participate in human communication. Because we are conditioned to the use of sight and sound, we tend to ignore using any other system. Most people also take it for granted, on the basis of common sense, that auditory symbols preceded visual symbols—that speaking preceded writing—in the development of language; indeed scholars generally agree that speech evolved before writing, although primitive pictorial communication may have developed quite early. The changes in the pronunciation and meaning of oral and written symbols have been and are being studied extensively in an attempt to help us understand how words develop. But at present the origins and development of language are largely matters of speculation.

Whatever the origin of language, efficient communication depends on the encoder's choice of code symbols that are meaningful to both encoder and decoder. The code symbol may be a single word or a series of words. But even when such symbols are common to the experience of both encoder and decoder and the native language is being spoken and the background and experiences are quite similar, meaning is elusive. If you are sitting in my living room and I say "chair" and point to a particular chair, we mutually share a specific reference. But if I describe the same chair without its being present, your image is likely to differ from mine no matter how thoroughly I describe the chair and how skillfully I use words. You will easily comprehend the meaning of "seat," "legs," and "back rest," but you will probably have an inaccurate picture of my specific chair. My code can have precise meaning for you only if you have seen my chair.

When we pass from the concrete to the conceptual, it is even less likely that the community of experience will suffice to fix meaning. Each individual has his own concept of "honesty," for example. For some it is determined principally by the act, for others principally by the motive behind the act. If a cashier gives a customer too much change, the customer may feel that it is not dishonest to keep the extra change because he did not plan to steal the money. Someone may copy a test answer that he saw by accident and still consider himself honest because he is only a passive receiver of stolen "goods." For some people honesty means anything you can get away with without public exposure. In such an instance standards depend on individual morality.

A teacher in an inner-city community college told his students that the lack of clarity in their communication was due to "lazy thinking." For his black students this was an immediate confirmation of the white man's stereotyping of the black man as shiftless and lazy. On the contrary, the instructor was using the phrase as it had been applied to him when he was a student by his teachers. Imagine the discrepancies in meaning that develop in the classroom as the vocabulary becomes more subjective and abstract. The symbols of language, then, go beyond being merely the means of processing the communication system; because they can mean so many different things to different people, they are part of the input into the system. This is the significance of Marshall McLuhan's epigram "The medium is the message."[1]

ACOUSTICS AND WORD ORDER

In addition to the choice of the symbol in spoken language other factors influence meaning as well: acoustics of language and word order. In considering these factors, one must bear in mind that language is primarily spoken and that written language is only an approximation of a verbal experience. To illustrate, answer the following four questions:

1. How many vowels are there in English?
2. How many consonants?
3. How do we detect a question in oral English?
4. In an American-English sentence how is meaning primarily conveyed?

From a representative group of students—and teachers—the following responses occur consistently and almost unanimously:

1. Five, sometimes six; they are *a, e, i, o, u,* sometimes *y.*
2. Twenty or twenty-one (depending upon the use of *y*).
3. The pitch rises at the end of a sentence.
4. Vocabulary.

In no instance is the response accurate. In the first and second answers both vowels and consonants should be primarily defined as sounds; the memorized responses offered are *letters.* What is the difference? Sounds refer to spoken language, letters to written language. Consider the difference in each of the following italicized syllables (a phonetic tran-

---

[1] Marshall McLuhan, *Understanding Media* (New York: McGraw-Hill, 1964).

scription of each syllable is provided to demonstrate graphically that each word contains a different vowel): *beat* [bit], *bit* [bɪt], *bait* [bet], *bet* [bɛt], *bat* [bæt], *bottom* ['batm], *bought* [bɔt], *boat* [bot], *boot* [but] *butch* [butʃ], *Bert* [bɝt], *but* [bʌt]. In each of these italicized words a change in *vowel sound* changes the meaning of the word; in ten of the twelve words the vowel change is the *only control* of meaning, since the vowel is preceded only by the sound [b] and followed only by the sound [t] in *ten* of *twelve* items. Clearly, American English—which contains all of these words listed—has *at least* twelve vowels. The sounds, not the letters, are of primary importance; likewise with consonants, of which there are many more than the twenty or twenty-one letters of the alphabet that might be listed.

The responses to the third question were equally inaccurate or, more precisely, incomplete. We do not generally detect a question in oral English by a pitch rise at the end of a sentence, nor is vocabulary item the only conveyor of meaning in English. Read the following questions aloud: How are you? Where are you going? What is the matter? When are you going? Why did you stop? Who is that? Is this good? This is good? In how many of these questions did pitch, or final intonation, rise to *denote* meaning? In the sentence just concluded did the pitch inside your head, in your inner ear, rise at the end of the sentence? If it did, was it necessary? Only one sentence intended as a question in this paragraph thus far requires pitch rise for denotative clarity as a question: This is good? All other questions included are structured as questions; the order of the words, *not* the question mark at the end of the sentence, identifies the sentence as a question. But in "This is good?" a declarative sentence, or a statement order, is used, and to indicate the interrogative, a question mark and a pitch rise are required. In all other sentences that are questions an initial word (who, why, what, where, when, how) followed by the verb, or action word, signaled the question pattern, or the positioning of the action word in the utterance signaled the question pattern (Is this good? . . . was it necessary?). For denotative meaning in an English question final intonation (pitch pattern) *must* rise only when the sentence structure is other than a question. Of course, for particular *connotative* meaning the pitch *may* rise at the end of *any* question structure. In the question "Why did you stop?" a pitch rise on "stop" provides a special, connotative meaning giving the word "stop" added significance, perhaps questioning this particular behavior in contrast to others, say, starting or continuing.

The response to the fourth question "In an American-English sentence how is meaning primarily conveyed?" is generally "vocabulary," individual words that can be defined for clarification. This response explains such traditional in-class activities as vocabulary tests at week's end and foreign language classes in which new lexical items once memorized from assigned lists seem to give immediate or additional security to the learner of the new language. But how many of these students ever achieve fluency in the foreign language? What we call fluency depends as much on word order and vocal intonation as it does on vocabulary.

To determine the critical conveyor of meaning in an English utterance, consider how and why meaning changes in the following sentences from a television campaign to control drug addiction:

> Will it turn you on?
> Or will it turn on you?

The key word for meaning is "on." What changes the meaning of the first question in the television slogan to the second? The answer is the word order in the sentence—where the particular word is placed. The appearance of the words, their spelling, remains the same. Only their placement changes. In the first sentence the colloquialism "turn on" suggests the drug experience and holds meaning here only if the object of the experience, "you," is interposed between the two words. In the second sentence "turn" becomes the action word, and "on" introduces the phrase of which "you" becomes the object. In reading this segment aloud, word order, clearly understood by the reader, carries the meaning that is specified further by the vocalized use of pitch (intonation pattern) and rate (perhaps pause) particularly. Take still another formation: Will you turn it on? A new word order carries new meaning. Here is another: You will turn it on? Although the words that can be defined, specifically "you," "turn," and "it," help the literalness of the meaning, it is really the word order that conveys the meaning. A useful experiment in communication training is a game in which nonsense syllables are substituted for recognized lexical items. Then it can be seen that the word order and vocal manipulation above carry all meaning and attitude. For example:

> The gloop blarps in the zoogy flatch.

"The" and "in" are not lexical items but function words in English, which help indicate grammatical relationships. Clearly, the nonsense sentence is an English language structure. The fact that we do not recognize the vocabulary items, the nonsense words, is of little consequence. We readily recognize the purpose each word serves; for example, the "gloop" is doing the "blarping." There is one "gloop," verified by the form "blarps," because the *s* at the end of "blarps" in English indicates the person doing the action. From this basic nonsense sentence the following possibilities, among others, are available in the English language:

> Did the gloop blarp in the zoogy flatch?
> The gloop will blarp in the zoogy flatch?
> Don't blarp in the zoogy flatch, gloop!
> Gloop, blarp in the zoogy flatch!
> The gloop blarped in the zoogy flatch?
> The gloop blarped in the zoogy flatch.

Practice saying the original nonsense sentence rapidly, loudly, with a harsh vocal quality at a consistently low pitch, with careful articulation and pronunciation. A particular connotative meaning will emerge *despite* the nonsense vocabulary, because of the structure of the sentence and the encoder's interpretation of the vocal delivery based on previous experience with English. Change the vocal attack: Speak very slowly, at a listenable projection level, with a forced nasality, slurring articulation and pronunciation. The connotative meaning changes. Clearly, the word order and the vocal rendition carry a major burden of meaning.

Denotation and Connotation

We have seen that even the most clear-headed attempt on the part of an encoder to make words convey specific meanings is bound to have only partial success. Words as code symbols depend on common experience between encoder and decoder, and the area of their common experience is likely at best to be very limited. Within this area encoder and decoder can usually agree on what we call a word's "denotative" meaning. But beyond this each will have a private area in which exist what we call "connotative" meanings. A word can trigger a series of emotional responses with varying intensities and shades of meaning depending upon the individual's experience with it. "Home" is an obvious example of a word that has a denotative core of meaning but which at the same time carries with it a set of feelings and reactions that differ widely in connotation from person to person. Other examples are easily discovered in everyday conversation and in literature. The following is an excerpt from a discussion about the Selective Service System and a volunteer army by two eighth-grade students studying the American political system:

First
Student: There won't be many people who want to volunteer.

Second
Student: I think there would be more people who want to volunteer because people don't like to be pushed around or into something.
They'd rather go out for it. There aren't as many hippies as
there are normal Americans.

It is the connotative use of the word "normal" in contrast to the word
"hippie" that is the focus of the second student's reply. He implies a value
judgment of a "normal" American as being one who is a good citizen and
who would volunteer for military service. Had he used the word "average" or the word "patriotic," the implication of the sentence would have
been vastly different. The choice of the word "normal" is a conscious or
unconscious attempt to conform to established American values. Denotative meanings, on the other hand, are generally dictionary meanings, and
though they may have found general agreement in terms of ordinary
usage, they too are subject to evolutionary change, ambiguity, and pecu-
liarities of use and interpretation. Think, for example, of how a non-
American decoder might be confused by the phrase "I really blew it."

Sometimes several descriptions of the same event will be based on
identical information, but because of the choice of words, an entirely
different message will be communicated. *The New York Times,* reporting
on the throng of fans who came to a Manhattan funeral chapel to pay
their last respects to the popular singer Judy Garland, had this to say:

> Her fans said good-by to Judy Garland yesterday. They arrived before
> dawn at the Frank E. Campbell Funeral Home and stood for hours behind
> police barricades—thousands of elderly women, weeping young men, teen-
> aged girls, housewives, nuns, priests, beggars, cripples, and hippies.

The New York *Daily News* was a bit more metaphoric:

> Judy Garland, who went through many a pot of gold but never found
> much lasting contentment this side of the rainbow, received a last tribute
> yesterday from the thousands who adored her. They came in four
> crowded lanes for a last glimpse of the songstress at Frank Campbell
> Funeral Chapel, Madison and 81st St.

The *Town Crier* of Westport, Connecticut, went on a hyperbolic binge:

> Judy Garland, with vibrant voice and twinkling feet stilled in death, made
> the last of her great New York comebacks Thursday—forever a star to the
> thousands who came to bid goodby. . . . And hold her last audience Judy
> truly did. They stood in long lines down Fifth Avenue and east on 81st

Street, patiently awaiting a brief glimpse of the 47-year-old actress who died in London. . . .[2]

In each of these descriptions the denotative elements are the same, but the individual journalist embroidered the event according to his own experience, taste, and his interpretation of the expectations of his readers. In the *New York Times* report a sense of the size of the crowd and its heterogeneous quality is communicated, whereas in the other two, it is the singer's personality that is glorified.

The following classroom example is similar to the excerpts from the three newspapers:

Teacher A: Have you considered spending the time remaining before lunch meeting with your small group?

Teacher B: My advice to you is to use the time remaining before lunch to meet with your small group.

Teacher C: If you were smart, you'd spend the time remaining before lunch meeting with your small group.

In all three instances the denotative input is the same; however, the feedback will vary to the degree that the student decoders interpret the phrases: "Have you considered," "My advice to you," and "If you were smart." The first centers on student responsibility, the second is a complementary encoder-decoder relationship, and the third threatens the intelligence of the students.

Word Choice in Oral Processing

There is much that a teacher can do to increase the efficiency of the processing of verbal language. He should analyze the language skills of the students in the communication system. In addition to recognizing that a word may carry connotative import, the teacher as facilitator will recognize that oral language is "time-bound." That is, the message must be decoded immediately and feedback established before the next stimulus arrives. In written communication the reader's mind may focus on another stimulus, but he can come back to the exact spot on the page. If the listener's mind wanders in response to the connotation of the words, there is no instant replay available. As a result, redundancy in the oral message is, within limits, desirable. Oral communication may also suffer because the encoder fails to code his message with enough of the symbolic references gained through common experiences of the encoder and decoder.

[2] Quotes are taken from June 27, 1969, editions of all three newspapers.

Here, an eighth-grader, through internal and external feedback, senses his lack of sufficient symbolic references and therefore uses the word "protest" five times to attempt to cover his deficiency:

> A protest vote is—you're voting for a person on a protest basis, like you're protesting something. Like McCarthy didn't win the nomination of the Democrats, and you're voting for McCarthy to protest the Democrats—protesting who they picked.

The only referent for someone who did not understand the concept already is the illustration. But this single instance is scarcely enough to communicate much or all that the concept "protest vote" implies. In all the foregoing examples the encoder's choice of words has been an important input into the system, not merely the means of conveying the message but a vital factor in the message—or the absence of a message—processed.

Not only does the encoder's word choice affect the message the decoder receives, but by means of feedback word choice also affects the encoder's subsequent input. Sometimes the effect on the encoder is greater than on the decoder of the message. In one sense the speaker is creating a subsystem of communication within himself as he listens to his choice of words. His subsystem is scanning the output of the system he initiated and adjusting to the desirability, from his point of view, of that output. As the initiator encodes his message, he generates feedback not only from his decoder but also from himself. Thus he adjusts his thinking in preparation for his next input in terms of two kinds of feedback, that which he receives from the listener and that which he receives from his own monitoring subsystem. Figure 3–1 shows how language is constantly influencing the message, while it is the vehicle for carrying it:

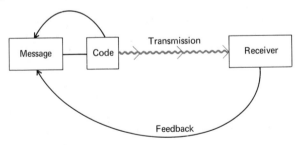

Fig. 3–1

In the following hypothetical situation notice how choice of words affects the functioning of the system and how feedback can result in changes in input:

Jimmy says, "Henry just took my pencil." Henry knows that Mary took the pencil, but he admires Mary, and so he decides not to "tell on her." Henry must decide what input he should add to the system; he must defend himself against a false accusation, but he cannot tell the whole story. He may say Jimmy is "wrong," "mistaken," "lying," or "stupid," among other possible input. But, the word Henry chooses will affect Jimmy's reaction and will also affect Henry's further input. Once Henry calls Jimmy a "liar," for instance, he will have to keep adding input to support his stated conviction that Jimmy is a liar. If the connotative meaning of the word "liar" is sufficiently damaging from Jimmy's life experience, it might provoke Jimmy to threaten a fist fight, whereas the word "stupid" may only produce further dialogue. The feedback to Henry of Jimmy's behavior will influence Henry's next input. If Henry does not want a fist fight, his own subsystem may initiate a change in input to modify his earlier labeling of Jimmy as a "liar"; if Henry does want a fight, he may repeat or reinforce the accusation. His subsequent language is based upon feedback and what his monitoring subsystem tells him is necessary to make the system function efficiently—that is, make it produce the desired behavior on Jimmy's part. Interestingly, the experimentation seems to indicate that teachers who identify students with particular intellectual groups tend to force these students to comply with predetermined expectations.

ORAL VERSUS WRITTEN COMMUNICATION

The following transcript of an elementary classroom session in a New York City school will further illustrate what we have been discussing. The purpose of the session is to compare the nature of written and oral communication. The children have previously written a composition, and each child is now to read his account and then tell the same story in conversational fashion.

Transcript	Comments
Teacher: O.K. Monday, a few of you wrote your stories. James: *(referring to the tape recorder)*: Can I turn this on? Teacher: No—just wait, please. And some of you were absent. Now what I'd like to do today—those	As the teacher presents these directions, there is no final drop in pitch to indicate the end of a sentence. There are word repetitions, phrases are incomplete, the contractions reinforce the spoken rhythms, the words are short, and the personal pronouns indicate oral code. (In written code this might

Transcript	**Comments**
of you who were absent to start writing the story. You won't have to write the whole thing. What I'd like you to do is just write the beginning. Once you get started and once you get the ideas organized—and once you know exactly what it is you want to say—all you have to do is write down some key words, some ideas that will remind you of the story. And I'll let you just tape the story. You won't have to write the whole thing.	read: Students who were absent should start to write some key words so that they can tell the story even if they missed the writing part of the assignment.) Notice how many times the teacher tells them that they do not have to write the whole story. She keeps encoding the message in response to feedback that tells her that the students are not perceiving the message.
Teacher: Let's see. Larry, here's yours. I'll ask you to read it. **Larry:** I have to write more? **Teacher:** No, you don't. That's good. **Larry:** Just this one. **Teacher:** The one you did on Monday. O.K. James? Who else? Who else was here? **Susie:** I was. **Teacher:** James, this is yours. **James:** I was—but I don't want to. **Teacher:** You have to. Who else was here? **Mary:** I wasn't here. **Teacher:** Yvonne is right here. O.K. Let's begin. You can begin now. **Larry:** I want to read mine first. **Teacher:** Please take off your coat. **Yvonne:** Larry did one already.	You can detect that the teacher is correct in her observation that the children did not understand her directions from the verbal feedback of questions. Part of the confusion stems from lack of clarity in her use of the code; however, this is quite typical of the giving of directions in oral fashion. The first time a message is encoded, the process can be very inefficient. After reading the teacher's wordy introduction sentence, the children's questions seem very clear. Each child is communicating with one person—the teacher. The teacher is attempting to encode a message that will cover all the possibilities of the group. That an oral message must be understood instantly is sometimes an advantage. It can be corrected instantly. The receiver of the mes-

Transcript	Comments
Teacher: But this is the second time. O.K. Go ahead. Oh, that's right, you wanted to show it to your teacher.	sage is there to demand clarification so that he can decode or delay the impact of the message. It is difficult to argue with a written direction—even if you don't understand it.
Larry: But I forgot.	
Billy: He lost it.	
Teacher: All right, will you do that now?	As yet, Larry has not read his story in spite of the directions given earlier. He can tell from the comments of the other students that they are not ready to listen to his message. Some of the absent students have not yet put the message together with anything in their previous experience. The mere repetition of instructions is equivalent to a foreign language. The teacher is still trying to find some common experiences.
Mary: What are you supposed to do?	
Teacher: You begin.	
Susie: Write the same one I wrote.	
Teacher: No, the second one. What you have to do— remember the first story we wrote.	
Peter: I wasn't here.	
Teacher: The first—the first story that I wrote on the big one. Weren't you with us then? Are you sure you weren't with us?	
Ann: No, he wasn't.	
Peter: I was absent four days.	Note the sentence structure of the children. Recent research in language patterns supports the hypothesis that language habits are established early in childhood. Children from lower economic backgrounds use the simple, direct sentence, whereas children from higher levels use sentence structures that reflect relationships of ideas.
Teacher: Right at the very beginning when we first started and I wrote the stories on the large piece of paper.	
Peter: No, I was sick.	
Teacher: O.K. This is what you are supposed to do. Think of something interesting that has happened to you. If you can't think of something interesting that has happened to you. If you can't think of something offhand, make something up and really use your imagination.	

Transcript	Comments
Billy: Oh, it hurts me.	When the child says, "It hurts me," he does not refer to physical pain but to his reaction to what the teacher has asked him to do. It is equivalent to the groan of the college student when an assignment is announced. The teacher ignores the comment because of the attitude of the speaker. If she read only the verbal message, she would have to stop to inquire the cause of the statement. The teacher knows from this last feedback that the students have at last understood what is expected.
Teacher: O.K. Larry, you read your story but—excuse me—now while he's reading just to hear what his voice sounds like—and to hear that when he reads something, he sounds a lot different than when he is just talking to me—and I'll show you how.	Now the teacher is explaining the purpose of the activity. The children can respond either by asking more questions—or by ignoring directions that they do not understand. (Do you understand the directions after reading them just one time?)
Mary: You don't hear your real voice.	The only child who responds makes a comment on "hearing your real voice." Other children go on with the business of finding a pencil. Perhaps, as far as they are concerned, the confusing statement of the teacher is so far beyond decoding that there is no need to ask a question. Often a quiet classroom or lack of questions means that the listener did not understand rather than that he comprehends perfectly the purpose of the speaker.
Ronnie: I don't have my pencil. I left mine.	We communicate with a purpose— we want a reward of changed behavior or the pleasure of understanding. A message that we do not
Teacher: You can use mine. You were told to bring a	

Transcript	Comments
pencil each time. (*Another child grabs the pencil.*) Ronnie: I had that pencil first. Teacher (*retrieving pencil*): All right, but you took it. He asked for it. Larry, go on. Do you have a title? Larry: Nope. Teacher: Think of one.	understand will force a quick change of subject.
Larry: I got it: "Stitch me." (*Reading*) When I was five years old, I was hit by a swing in Central Park. I got three stitches. I was in the hospital for a few days, and when I got out of the hospital, I couldn't—I couldn't had to stay in bed, and I couldn't go outside to play for two weeks. When my sister was eight years old, my mother took us—took me and my sister to the park, and she was riding her bicycle down the hill —she fell off the bike and cut her leg. She had to go to the hospital. She couldn't walk for a few weeks.	Note the change in sentence structure and the very stiff and measured rhythm of the written account. Larry's English teacher might have been pleased with this evidence that Larry could write very close to "acceptable" standard patterns. Certainly any reader could follow the chronological sequence of thought.
Teacher: That's good, now. You read that really well. Teacher: Now tell the story without reading it. What happens here?	
Larry: Well, see I was walking through—you know— where the swings was— and this little kid who was pumping real hard —I was walking in back of the swings—like I	As Larry tells the story of what happened, the code becomes more vivid and specific. There are more details. A written speech will have more clarity but less immediacy than a spontaneous speech.

Transcript	Comments

was walking near the fence—and he was pumping so high, he hit me on my (*pointing*) right over here.

Ann: Did it hurt?

Larry: Yeah! What d'ya think? It hurt, I got three stitches. There's still two of them.

Billy: I saw them.

Larry: There's two right here.

Peter: How does them stitch you up?

Teacher: Larry, go on.

Mary: I don't know what to write.

Note the subsystem of communication during the pause.

Susie: I know— I write one to my teacher.

Larry: And then they took me to the hospital. And I had to get in bed—and later on they put me to sleep. I don't know how they did it.

Larry's vocal quality indicates deep involvement in the situation. When he read what he had written, he was slow and careful. His voice told the audience that this was most mysterious and wonderful.

Mary: O.K.

Larry: But they just put me to sleep—stitched that up.

Yvonne: Like my brother—he got hit by a car—he got three stitches.

Teacher: You have to be careful —you're interrupting.

Larry: That's all— Wait a minute. You want to know what happened to my sister? They put some kind of nose that you could sleep—and then when you're asleep, they take the thing off, and they start doing it with oxygen tank.

Larry likes all the feedback to his message. He is adapting his content to what his audience finds interesting. However, he is now coding his ideas as he goes along. He doesn't have time to search for an accurate word, so he uses "thing." Confusion is started by Larry's unusual language structure, which causes misinterpretation by the teacher.

Transcript	Comments
Teacher: Oxygen tent—does that put you out?	She introduces a new term, and Larry attempts to clarify.
Larry: No, that's what they put you in. No, they give you some kind of stuff to make you go to sleep. When I was little, I almost died.	Larry is not getting the reaction that he expected. He considers "die" an important shock word. He has a limited vocabulary of shock words, so he had to repeat the same word, each time increasing the force of his voice.
Teacher: Is it a liquid or a pill?	
Larry: When I was four, I almost died.	
Teacher: An injection?	Finally the rest of Larry's audience gets his message, even though the teacher does not add the strong connotation to the word held by the children. His listeners begin to encode in the same style.
Larry: Yeah. I was so little, I wouldn't remember. When I was—a little baby, I almost died.	
Mary: How?	
Ann: Me too.	
Teacher: Glad you made it, Larry. (*Just a tiny bit of sarcasm*)	
Ronnie: Me too.	
Larry: When I was little.	
Billy: I almost got hit.	
Larry: I had an asthma attack. When I was two weeks old.	
Peter: When I was born, I was retarded. (*Said with great pride*)	The encoding confusion here is not unusual at this grade level. However, this misuse of "retarded" produced great mirth in the class. Certain words have strong emotional connotations, and the speaker picked one that produced strong listener reaction.
Teacher: No, I don't think so. Do you know what that means? (*Laughter from the group*)	
Peter: No. weak—awful weak.	
Teacher: That's not retarded. I think the word you want is anemic.	
Peter: Minemic?	
Teacher: Anemic.	
Yvonne: No—you know what happened to my sister. She was riding down—	

Transcript	Comments
Larry (*loudly*): I'm going to kill somebody in a minute.	Larry tries to use the code again to focus attention on himself. But even
Ronnie: All right, turn it off, turn it off.	the word "kill" does not seem to be effective. Although the teacher
Peter (*to teacher*): Are you anemic?	says she believes him, her processing belies the verbal code, and it
Teacher: I hope not.	would appear that only Larry himself believes his threat.
Larry (*to teacher*): Don't you believe me?	
Teacher: I do believe you, but I hope you don't do it.	

This transcript indicates that the initial purpose of the lesson, to compare written and oral communication, was not realized; however, the classroom encounter demonstrates what can develop in a communication system when the facilitator does not sufficiently guide the processing of the less sophisticated participants. Here the teacher continually allowed subsystems to emerge that were neither fulfilled nor organized to support the main system. Larry was forced to emotionalize his code to attract attention to the subsystem between him and the teacher. Meanwhile the teacher was attempting to deal with all the other subsystems, until eventually the total communication system disintegrated. The efficient facilitator will use enough denotative input to control the processing without limiting imaginative student participation. His contribution to the encounter must be specific so as to maintain the intended communication design without its developing into a linear pattern that elicits self-limiting automatic responses from the student.

Four

Nonverbal Behavior

Verbal language is the most easily isolated input into a communication system. The words and grammatical structures are identifiable as written or oral symbols with definable limits of meaning. But there is another significant input into the system: the nonverbal behavior that either accompanies verbal communication or stands alone. The nonverbal message is carried by components of voice, facial expressions, bodily gestures, appearance, posture, and spatial relationships with the other members of the communication system. This nonverbal behavior can amplify, support, modify, or even provide clues that contradict the speaker's verbal message. Thus nonverbal behavior can never be discounted as an important element of the input into the system.

One axiom of communication, as stated in the book *Pragmatics of Human Communications,* is: *"One cannot* not *communicate."*[1] That is, man is communicating even when he does not wish to send a message to a receiver, for all observable behavior is communication. The teacher in the classroom may communicate his level of physical energy by the way he walks into the classroom. The student's nonverbal behavior tells the teacher how the student feels about himself, gives meaning to environmental conditions at the moment, and is a major source of feedback pertaining to the success of the communication system.

[1] Paul Watzlawick, Janet Helmick Beavin, Don D. Jackson, *The Pragmatics of Human Communications* (New York: Norton, 1967), pp. 48 ff.

DIFFERENCES BETWEEN NONVERBAL
AND VERBAL COMMUNICATION

In his article "Communication Without Words" Albert Mehrabian offers a formula for the "total impact" of a communication; this formula is based on the verbal, vocal, and facial factors.[2] The devised Mehrabian formula is: "Total Impact = .07 verbal + .38 vocal + .55 facial." The 7 percent devoted to the literal words and grammar, the linguistic habits, may seem extraordinarily low. However, the authors of *The First Five Minutes* substantiate Mehrabian's findings (if not his exact figures) when, through the device of the "microscopic interview," they indicate that the paralinguistic—the vocal and the facial—elements of a communication are extremely influential in the processing and decoding of a message. In *The First Five Minutes* it is stated:

> The [paralinguistic habits] show variation from culture to culture and from region to region. They are as much the product of experience as are one's language habits. Furthermore, they clearly perform a communicative function. *Go away!* said in a low, slow, soft and stern "tone of voice" can be more frightening than the same words screamed angrily at the top of the lungs.[3]

These concepts are explored in subsequent chapters. Here we are concerned with the visual aspects of nonverbal communication.

Nonverbal behavior in communication differs from verbal behavior in degree rather than in kind; there are commonalities between the two forms in spite of their differences. Both are arbitrary and symbolic, though nonverbal communication to a lesser degree. At times nonverbal behavior can be more spontaneous than verbal behavior. Both reflect the culture and environment in which they occur. Efficiency in reading both codes depends on the backgrounds of the encoder and decoder and their common experiences.

Verbal and nonverbal behavior can be involuntary as well as voluntary, although verbal language tends to be largely voluntary and nonverbal communication involuntary. The so-called Freudian slips and other automatic linguistic responses cannot be dismissed totally, but for the most part our verbal responses are under our conscious control. Nonverbal gestures used to communicate a specific concept—for example, a numeri-

[2] Albert Mehrabian, "Communication Without Words," *Psychology Today*, 2 (September 1968), pp. 53–55.
[3] Robert E. Pittenger, Charles F. Hockett, John J. Danehy, *The First Five Minutes* (Ithaca: Paul Martineau, 1960), p. 23a.

cal value indicated by holding up a specified number of fingers for the viewer to count—are clearly voluntary, but more often a gesture such as stroking the hair or fingering a tie is not planned or controlled.

Verbal symbols, too, carry both connotative and denotative meaning, and usage determines which is more important in a communicative encounter. Nonverbal behavior, however, can sometimes be coded so as to carry denotative meaning, but usually its meaning is less specific and therefore more connotative. A coded nonverbal system can carry factual information, but in human interaction the usual carrier of such messages is verbal language, nonverbal behavior serving as an ancillary agent leaking information that might not otherwise be revealed.

Such leakage of information can affect communication in many ways. It can, for example, be a clue to a deception that may or may not be deliberate, for the encoder does not always know that he is in the act of dissembling. As an example, consider the bride's father who before the wedding insists, in all honesty, that he is not apprehensive about his role in the ceremony as he paces nervously about the room. As the encoder of this message of apprehension, he is the only one being deceived, for though he may have convinced himself of the truth of his verbal message, his observers are well aware of the tension he is experiencing. Here the observer-decoder is receiving the more accurate message. As human communication becomes more involved, other kinds of deception can be practiced: There may be interaction in which the encoder is perpetrating a deception on himself as well as his decoder, so that neither is aware of the true nature of the communication. For example, in recounting a painful experience, a child, though seeming pleased to tell the story, is hesitant in his delivery because of unhappy associations. His listener interprets the hesitancies as being related to a speech defect or lack of fluency with language. The child is not aware of conflicts in telling the story, and the listener ascribes the child's behavior to a permanent affliction rather than a temporary unsettled state.

Nonverbal communication can be divided into two major categories, based on the processing characteristic of the message: those messages that, after processing, are received by the ears and interpreted by auditory centers of the central nervous system; and those received by the other senses, primarily those received by the eyes and decoded by visual centers of the central nervous system. The encoder's manipulation of the elements of speech greatly influences the decoder's reception of the verbal code; and it is the visual, kinesthetic, and tactile messages that the layman usually means when he refers to nonverbal communication.

FACIAL EXPRESSIONS AND GESTURES

The largest class of purely nonverbal messages consists of those conveyed by facial movements and expressions. The face and particularly the eyes generally receive careful scrutiny by the decoder while he is absorbing the verbal message. The speaker who does not look at his listener may prevent such scrutiny, but he does this at the expense of conveying another nonverbal message: fear that his face or eyes will convey a nonverbal message he does not want read. There is substantial evidence to support the theory that, in many cases in which a person is convinced he is in control of his facial gestures, he is actually sending subliminal messages about his attitudes and emotional states. For instance, a face that, to the casual observer, appears to be conveying cordiality to those around him will reveal, when analyzed by means of a high-speed motion picture film, instantaneous flashes of hostility around the corners of the mouth and the region of the eyes. Such fleeting messages have been labeled micromomentary facial expressions and may account for the uneasiness or lack of trust that some speakers engender without having any obvious grounds for such reactions.

According to the studies done by experimental psychologists Paul Ekman and Wallace Friesen, facial expressions communicate the type of emotion that the sender is experiencing, while the body and, in particular, the hands and feet tell the observer something about the intensity of the emotion.[4] The teacher who is attentive to the degree of tension evidenced in a student's hand movements and the amount of such activity will receive valuable information about the student's mental set. Gestures that involve the hands or other movable parts of the anatomy can, in addition to giving information about one's emotional state, also be a conscious pantomiming of an action to give information that cannot be conveyed by other means or clarified by verbal messages. There are several kinds of such gestures. The librarian who puts her index finger to her lips in the standard gesture for silence without making a sound is using a form of nonverbal behavior known as an emblem. If the gesture is accompanied by the words "Be quiet," it becomes an illustrator or amplifier for the verbal message. The same gesture can be a regulator in a conversation when it is used by a speaker to indicate to his listener that he is not finished and does not wish to be interrupted. One further kind of gesture is not related to pantomime. Some facial movements and gestures provide

[4] Paul Ekman and Wallace V. Friesen, "The Repertoire of Nonverbal Behavior: Categories, Origins, Usage, and Coding," *Semiotica,* Vol. 1, No. 1 (1969), pp. 49–98.

satisfaction for the individual without conveying information—stroking one's hair or blinking one's eyes serve only to relieve tension and are called adapters.

APPEARANCE AND BODILY ENERGY

A second kind of visual code is the overall appearance and bodily energy of the speaker. The style in which an individual dresses is, of course, the result of conscious choice; however, the motivation for making a particular selection is the result of individual needs. In addition, the manner in which he wears clothes, his energy level, and his muscle tension give involuntary clues about his feelings. Studies indicate that very few people are successful at masking their bodily responses and deceiving their observers.[5] A controlled voice and a smiling face may be betrayed by shifting feet and clenched fists. As a general rule, we judge the level of involvement and interest in communication of a speaker by the appropriateness of the degree of tension of his body. We interpret too little bodily energy as a sign of lack of interest in the message and too much energy as a sign that the speaker is suffering from fear of the message or the communication encounter. This kind of feedback obviously serves as input into the system, for the sensitive observer adjusts or recalibrates his message to allay the fear; if fear is the response he wants, of course, he may intensify his message.

Perhaps our chief means of understanding this code is kinesthetic rather than visual: That is, the observer feels the same type of muscle tension as the speaker. For example, if you attend a play that affects you deeply, at the end of the evening your muscles may actually ache as if you had been through as much physical exertion as the actors on stage. Likewise, while listening to someone who speaks with an exceedingly tense voice, the listener may feel the muscles in his own vocal mechanism tighten. These muscular responses on the part of the receiver of nonverbal messages enter into the system and affect his input and processing.

A certain amount of bodily tension is helpful in projecting a feeling of involvement and compels the receiver of the message also to become involved or at least interested in the progress of the system. In the classroom system the posture of the students is one of the most important feedbacks a teacher receives, for it gives him a reading of the students' interest in the activity and the strength of the motivation to participate.

[5] Dean Barnlord reports such studies in *Interpersonal Communication: Survey and Studies* (Boston: Houghton Mifflin, 1968), pp. 511–613.

ENVIRONMENTAL SETTING AND PERSONAL SPACE

The environmental settings and the opportunities they provide for interactions also affect the processing of the communication system. The kind
and number of relationships that develop in a class that is arranged in
small groups or circles will be different from those developed in classes
whose desks are in straight lines. In the more formal setup the child
cannot communicate freely and naturally with his classmates. The freedom of the "open classroom" does much to create an atmosphere in which
students can learn to relate to their peers. Also, the child who must
always sit at a level lower than the teacher's will perceive the teacher
quite differently from the child who often sits level with the teacher.
Although few of us think about this consciously, the teacher reveals his
own identification of his role as symmetrical or complementary to the
students by his "geographic" position in the classroom. A teacher will tell
his class how he feels about them by where he stands or sits as the
students enter the room. For example, if he stands in a far corner and
watches them come in, he has implied that he will be distant, whereas by
standing at the door to greet them, the teacher tells the students that he is
glad and willing to share the environment. If the teacher pulls back as
students approach, he communicates the same message of distance and
possibly rejection.

In his book *The Hidden Dimension* the anthropologist Edward Hall
develops the theory that each individual has a "personal space" in which
he operates.[6] The amount of space an individual marks off for himself
and the degree of freedom with which he allows others to enter his space
are determined largely by his cultural background. In most European
countries shaking hands is the accepted mode of greeting and taking
leave; however, in the United States, this contact is generally reserved
only for introductions and is avoided on other occasions. Like nudity,
invasion of personal space has been used by some groups for shock value.
For example, the Living Theatre deliberately violated the established
convention that actors do not have physical contact with members of the
audience, as a means of ensuring involvement on the part of the audience.

Most research on spatial relationships has been done on seating arrangements in a group. For example, Rosenfeld discovered that strangers
who sought to affiliate tended to choose seating about five feet from each
other, while those who wished to remain distant from one another were
seated about eight feet apart.[7] Other findings have indicated that more

[6] Edward T. Hall, *The Hidden Dimension* (Garden City, N.Y.: Doubleday, 1966).
[7] H. Rosenfeld, "Effect of Approval-Seeking Induction on Interpersonal Proximity,"
Psychological Reports (1965), pp. 17, 120–122.

FIGURE 4–1   In most cultures in order for real involvement
to take place among individuals, it is necessary for the
participants to face each other or at least approximate this
position. In the picture of the bench sitters the person who
is more involved in communicating with the other individual
is the woman who is attempting to establish a face-to-face
encounter. The other woman demonstrates her degree of
interest in the speaker and her message by maintaining an
appropriate position. Contrast this picture with that of the
college students in discussion with Vice-President Agnew.

IN FIGURE 4–2 The long-haired male student's extreme
position and the placement of his feet indicate that he would
probably stand to confront the Vice-President if he were
permitted to do so. The other two students seem to be
withdrawn from the immediate confrontation: The male
leans away as far as possible within his personal space; the
female focuses within herself. With the bench sitters we see
how the angle of confrontation projects the willingness of
each to participate. The one on the right is more willing to
be involved in this encounter.

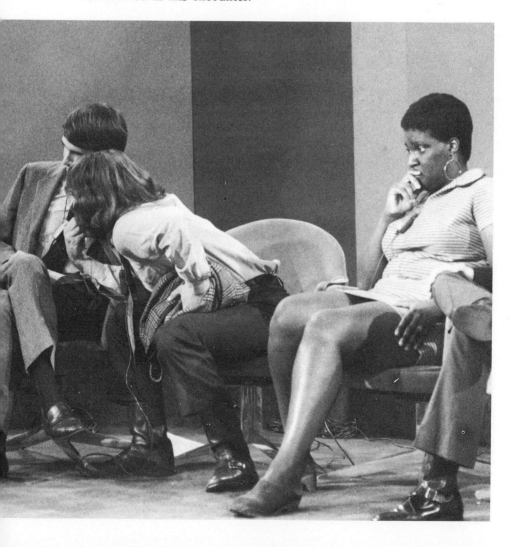

FIGURE 4-4 This child is obviously involved in his internal world; he ignores external stimuli. His level of body tension and the position of his body provide information regarding the relative serenity of his thoughts, even though he is not attempting to communicate his personal, internal involvement to the external world.

FIGURE 4-3 The policeman attempts to comfort the unhappy child by kneeling down to the boy's level in order to establish a direct face-to-face relationship and by extending a hand and touching the child in order to provide a protective cover.

FIGURE 4–5 Facial tension and hand gesture provide clues for the observer as to the nature and intensity of emotion experienced by the young man in this montage.

FIGURE 4–6 *"One cannot not communicate."*

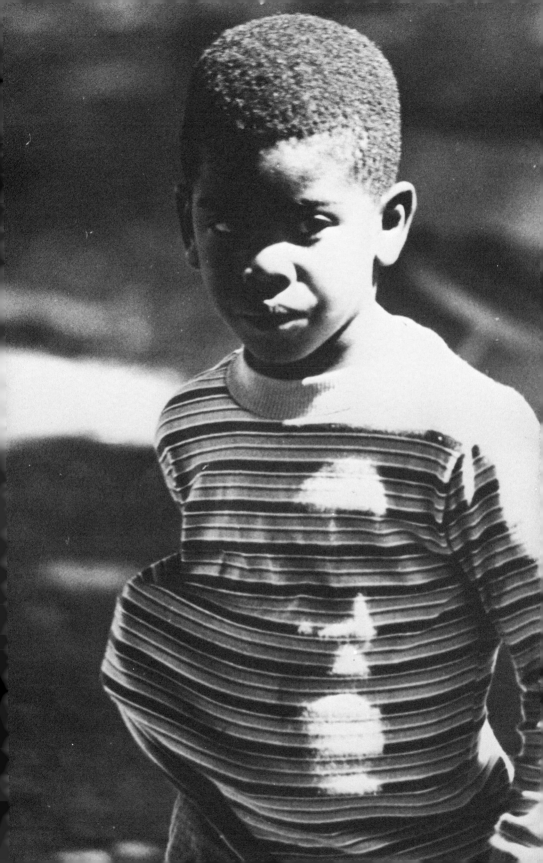

FIGURE 4–7 Can the decoder question the mutual dislike
of the two participants in this encounter? Is a verbal
message necessary?

communication occurs when people sit opposite each other than when they are next to each other. But solid conclusions are extremely difficult in this area because there are so many factors involved. For example, if X and Y are close to each other and opposite each other, but not facing each other, they will not interact as much as A and B, who are far apart but facing each other. Distance is one factor and direction the other. In one case the two people may be separated by direction even though the space between them is less.

Movement within personal space is also a factor in conveying a message. We move toward a person to influence him to come into balance with our opinion but retreat when we do not wish to accept his view. The exaggerated behavior of the melodramatic actor in looking away and extending the arm is a stylized version of this phenomenon. A child spontaneously moves close to the teacher with whom he wishes to interact and identify and away from someone he regards as unpleasant. In groups in which close relationships and lack of inhibitions are important to the functioning of the group, nonverbal exercises—touching and stroking— are used to invade the personal space of the group members in order to speed up the "breaking-the-ice" process.

Everyone does not have the same ability to read nonverbal cues. There is some evidence to support the hypothesis that sensitive observers may be trained in such reading ability by the use of films, video tapes, and practice in small groups. A teacher should take every opportunity to sharpen his ability to read nonverbal messages as well as to check the nonverbal messages he is sending to his class.

The photographic essay beginning on page 58 illustrates various types of nonverbal cues and the effects of spatial relationships on interpersonal communication.

Five

Perceptual Behavior

Time: Dinnertime
Place: At the dining table
Characters: Bride of three months and husband

HUSBAND: What made you cook chicken livers for dinner tonight?

BRIDE: Because you like them.

HUSBAND: But I don't like them.

BRIDE: But you ate them when we had them at the Smiths' buffet last weekend.

HUSBAND: Yes, but that was at the Smiths', and besides I don't like them well enough to have chicken livers twice in the same week.

BRIDE: I don't understand you. You helped yourself, they were not served to you. Why would you take something you don't like? I don't understand you. . . .

The above scene has no doubt been played many times, perhaps not always at dinner tables or between a husband and wife. Yet the basic situation of one individual misinterpreting the behavior of another individual and ascribing meaning—not the intended meaning—to this behavior is a major cause for breakdown in countless numbers of communication systems and subsystems. One individual receives a message but in processing the message may distort it to fit his own feeling at the time or his previous experience. In the domestic scene illustrated here the bride assumes that her husband's eating of chicken livers at the Smiths' buffet meant that he liked them and would enjoy having the same meal at home. She does not take into account the fact that social pressures might have been working on her husband so that he felt obliged to taste all the dishes at the buffet. She might have, because of a great passion for chicken livers herself, seized on this behavior and used it so that she could justify cooking chicken livers for herself. Whether the husband's behavior was inconsistent or the bride was acting on the basis of her own food preferences, her *perception* of her husband's food preferences was not accurate.

THE ACT OF PERCEIVING

The act of perceiving involves all the senses, though it is usually the visual and auditory senses that are the dominant organs delivering messages to the brain for interpretation. How we interpret or perceive the messages we receive is related to our previous experiences with the same or at least similar experiences, our ability to interpolate across experiences, and our emotional state at the time. Perception is a very personal thing, for it exists within the individual and is what happens to messages or stimuli after they are internalized. It is largely an unconscious process. Renato Tagiuri and Luigi Petrullo in their book *Person Perception and Interpersonal Behavior* write of person perception in the following way (italics theirs):

> Indeed, when we speak of person perception or of knowledge of persons, we refer mostly to the observations we make about *intentions, attitudes, emotions, ideas, abilities, purposes, traits*—events that are, so to speak, inside the person.[1]

In the early days of experimental psychology researchers concerned themselves with studies of how the sensory organisms received the messages from the outside sources. Later they became interested in what happened after the messages entered the brain. Our concern will be with this latter aspect as it would apply to classroom interaction, for a knowledge and recognition of the effects on the perceptual process, if applied to the communication system, can greatly aid in understanding and avoiding communication breakdowns.

[1] Renato Tagiuri & Luigi Petrullo (eds.), *Person Perception and Interpersonal Behavior* (Stanford, Cal.: Stanford University Press, 1958), p. x.

ESTABLISHING THE STIMULUS

We make two important assumptions about the kind of stimuli we receive through the scanning of messages. The first is that the message (or stimuli) we receive through the senses must be recognizable, distinctive, and repeatable in new settings. I assume that if I hear the patterns of sound frequencies that constitute the vowel in the word "bee," I can recognize the same pattern when I hear it again. I also assume that in American English there is a distinctive difference between the vowel in "see" and the vowel in "saw" and that I can discriminate between these sounds. The same two characteristics can be illustrated with colors: We assume that drivers of cars can recognize the red light at different street corners to mean "stop" and the green light to mean "go" and that the light-reflection characteristics of red are quite distinct from the light-reflection characteristics of green. Furthermore, we assume that once we have established the stimulus, its subsequent effects will be the same. When I smell a steak cooking over charcoal, I assume that the next time I smell that odor it will be coming from a steak (or at least beef) cooking over charcoal. When I see a smile on a person's face as an indication of friendliness, I assume that a smile on another face also means friendliness. The linear or lecture method of teaching depends upon this assumption of repeatability of stimuli to produce a specific outcome: that the information we present to one student that results in learning can be presented to other students with the same outcome. This teaching strategy becomes less reliable as we move from the concrete to the abstract, from the denotative to the connotative. An input of red and green lights demands the specific behavior of stopping and going, but the yellow light suggesting the abstraction "caution" requires that the decoder assess his situation and therefore creates difficulties in responding.

SIMILARITY OF SENSE IMPRESSIONS

The second assumption is that when I receive a sensory impression, another human being receives the same sensation. Although there is no such thing as a unity of sensory experience, there is similarity in the response to stimuli. When I stroke the fur on a rabbit, I assume that the sense experience that I have in my fingers is similar to the one you have when you stroke the same animal. When I hear the word "radish," I see a particular vegetable with definite characteristics, and I assume that you see a similar visual image.

Although the ear and the open eye are constantly scanning or survey-ing the environment, the brain is selective in the information it processes. The information is sorted into a memory bank established by previous experience. The receiver may actually supplement what he hears or sees with information from his mental storehouse, so that he can produce a pattern of meaning. Because of the physical nature of sound transmission by telephone, for example, many of the speech sounds are not carried to the receiver. But these sounds are not missed by the listener because he "fills in" the missing sounds, thus making the message comprehensible.

The brain is much like the computer in the speed with which it can select and combine information and compare it with data stored in its memory bank. Even though the senses may be focused to ignore certain stimuli, they are constantly scanning the field in which they are set. When we go to sleep, our ears are not turned off for certain sounds. A sleeper who is acclimated to living next door to a firehouse may ignore several noisy departures of the engines during the night but will be awakened by a slight noise at the door of his room. By constant exposure a parent becomes accustomed to the intensity level of the teen-ager's radio; how-ever, as soon as the intensity increases or decreases, the parent hears the sound that he had not noticed before. His scanner is set to notice differ-ences in the sound environment.

THE LIGHT WITHIN

In the scene at the beginning of this chapter the bride was scanning the entire environment for information about her husband's choice of food and storing it for use at a later date. She probably had other behaviors for storage as well, but for some reason, perhaps her own food preferences or despair with menu planning, she accentuated this particular behavior and interpreted it to mean that her husband liked chicken livers. Scanning the environment, selecting particular sensory stimuli, accentuating certain data through a perhaps unconscious predisposition, and interpreting the data in terms of past experiences are the essential activities for percep-tion. The psychologist Gordon Allport describes generalized concept-perception in the following paragraph:

> Nothing that strikes our eyes or ears conveys this message directly to us. We always select and interpret our impressions of the surrounding world. Some message is brought to us by the "light without" but the

meaning and significance we give to it are largely added by the "light within."[2]

What accounts for the various shadings of the "light within" is essential to understanding the effects of one's perceptual processes on the communication. In some cases a single unrelated subsystem may cause someone to select and interpret stimuli in a particular way. For example, a young man has a particularly unhappy experience with a young woman. After several months have passed, he meets another young woman who has similar coloring and the same hair style and dresses in the same mode as the first young woman. The young man rejects the new girl and is extremely rude to her, not because he really dislikes the second girl. He has no data with which to make this kind of judgment but is rejecting a "class" or category of female that caused him pain. Teachers might have an analogous experience involving two children from the same family. If the teacher had an antipathy for the older child in the family, he may find it very difficult to recognize good traits in the younger child.

This analogy can be extended to the treatment of ethnic groups. A second reading of the transcript of the discussion of "black power" in Chapter Two will reveal many instances in which responses to various statements might well be responses to earlier experiences rather than to the immediate discussion. One wonders if Peter's rejection of many of Gerri's ideas is really based on the evidence she is presenting or on that fact that she is black. Peter may be rejecting Gerri because she is a girl stating a point of view he does not accept from girls, black or otherwise. The volatile subject being discussed intensifies the relationship; those observing the dyadic interaction (between Peter and Gerri) may perceive Peter's behavior as racial when in fact it is sexual. The most obvious explanation for perceptual behavior may be the least pertinent.

Likewise we might better understand Gerri's seeming refusal to accept the white students' point of view if we knew more specifically about her past interactions with whites. She underscores her distrust in her rejection of the white man's media and her feeling that the white students will never understand her point of view. In her appraisal of Stokely Carmichael Gerri recounts her special understanding of his personality, since they share similar backgrounds, and then she says: "And don't tell me he hasn't had the back of many hands!" Here she is saying that Stokely Carmichael's view of the world is the result of the treatment he has received from the white man. Is Gerri assuming that Carmichael and she

[2] Gordon Allport, *The Nature of Prejudice* (Garden City, N.Y.: Doubleday Anchor Book, 1958), p. 161.

have received the same treatment from whites? Is she assuming that the white students in the classroom are behaving as the white media have behaved? We can never really answer these questions for the answers are determined by the "light within." How one perceives a message is one more input into the already complex communication system.

Another example of the distortion of perception affecting the treatment of ethnic groups appears in *The Vertical Ghetto.* Here are the words of a middle-aged black woman. But we must remember in reading the monologue that this represents a black's perception of the white's perception of the black world; also, note that the black woman speaking includes her perceptions of other minority groups, the Jews, that participate in her personal world:

> They [social workers, resident advisors] are always sending women to me and I'm supposed to show them how I keep house or prepare meals for my children. That's a joke! The average one of these women can cook me under the table and knows more about keeping a house clean than I will ever learn. Trouble is—they are always talking to the people down here and *nobody ever listens to them.* You forget—these are the women who have kept the city's homes clean for generations; they have fed the most prominent citizens and have kept the clothes on their backs starched and ironed. The crowned heads from the world over have eaten menus prepared by them. They have had closer contact with the children of their employers than the parents have. Trying to tell these people about things like that is like telling fish how to swim. No, it's something else these people need—and it's not telling them how to plan a menu. Seems to me you got to find some kind of way to make them take pride in themselves and what they do. You also got to find some way to keep the human scavengers from taking advantage of them. Look at all them little Jew credit stores up and down O Street—they take advantage of the people. A $5 pair of shoes cost $10, and by the time you get them paid for they cost $15 and they're already worn out. [Brackets and italics the author's][3]

The Vertical Ghetto provides an example of a child's perception of his parent. The book's author, William Moore, Jr., writes:

> The black boy . . . often views his father as an individual with a low-status job who does not exemplify the culturally projected image of the

[3] William Moore, Jr., *The Vertical Ghetto* (New York: Random House, 1969), p. 131.

fathers he views on television or sees in his textbooks. He constantly sees his father as an object of derision and indifference and not as a desirable figure to emulate. Perceiving his mother in an essential role in the home and his father as one who cannot adequately assume his position, the black boy sometimes develops a kind of role blur that makes nebulous his perception of what his own role should be:

"All we hear about is how important a father is, about going to church together—but that don't mean us. My daddy says the bosses on his job call him boy and he's forty-five years old. My momma can make more money than he can. He gets so mad that sometimes I don't see him for weeks. I don't know what they want you to say when people ask you, 'Don't you want to be like your daddy?' *I don't know what he's like.* [Italics the author's][4]

PERCEPTUAL DISTORTIONS IN LITERARY CHARACTERS

Literature, as a distillation of life's experiences, provides examples of characters whose distorted perception results in unexpected but inevitable and often tragic consequences. Perception distortion was responsible for the murder of Desdemona; Oedipus symbolically put out his eyes after the shocking realization of his inaccurate perceptions. In *Hedda Gabler* the prevailing society's most respectable representative, Judge Brack, concludes the Ibsen drama after Hedda's suicide by "half-falling in the arm-chair" and uttering the play's last line: "Good God!—people don't do such things." People do!—but not in Brack's perception.

American poet Edwin Arlington Robinson likewise dealt with perception distortion in many of the human beings he created as *The Children of the Night.* "Richard Cory" was one of these "children":

> Whenever Richard Cory went down town,
> We people on the pavement looked at him:
> He was a gentleman from sole to crown,
> Clean-favored, and imperially slim.
>
> And he was always quietly arrayed,
> And he was always human when he talked;
> But still he fluttered pulses when he said,
> "Good-morning," and he glittered when he walked.

4 *Ibid.,* pp. 71–72.

And he was rich—yes, richer than a king,
And admirably schooled in every grace:
In fine, we thought that he was everything
To make us wish that we were in his place.

So on we worked, and waited for the light,
And went without the meat, and cursed the bread;
And Richard Cory, one calm summer night,
Went home and put a bullet through his head.[5]

"We people on the pavement" perceived Richard Cory through eyes and ears accustomed to hardship, longing for relief. What they saw and heard—his physical movement, his regal appearance, his demonstrated taste, his speech, his money—they interpreted as demonstrating Richard Cory's happiness; his verbal and nonverbal messages led "we people" to think that "he was everything to make us wish that we were in his place." All the participants in the communication system or subsystems described in the poem are "children" who are victims of their own particular perceptual "night" and therefore not prepared to accept "a bullet through his head."

The following suggestions are ways of taking advantage of perceptual subsystems and getting more messages through to the students in a classroom. They can be useful to the teacher only to the extent that the teacher is perceptive and fulfills his role as facilitator—that is, he must so thoroughly understand his listener and sense the other's feelings that he can phrase and articulate a message to the needs of his listener.

1. An encoder scans his environment for messages that affect his immediate well-being. Sometimes he scans to escape injury or pain; other times he anticipates pleasure or reward. Sometimes he scans so that he can determine how he can be accepted by the group. Subject matter that relates to the needs, habits, roles, or desires of the listener will gain attention from the scanning process. Some researchers call this "salience." High school students will find the topics of "required courses" and "compulsory class attendance" far more salient to their well-being than a discussion of Social Security. However, this does not mean that the teacher must be restricted to topics that he judges immediately appropriate to his students in his classroom in his city at a certain time on a specific day. But when he chooses a topic that is removed from the immediate environment, the message must have salience. The plight of the Irishman

---

[5] "Richard Cory" is reprinted by permission of Charles Scribner's Sons from *The Children of the Night* by Edwin Arlington Robinson (1897).

during the potato famine of 1846 may be applicable to the life of the indigent ghetto dweller in New York in the 1970s, but this will only be apparent to the students if the teacher appropriately facilitates an understanding of the relationship.

2. The encoder scans for information that agrees with his attitudes and previous views. He tends to ignore the stimuli that cause imbalance; or else he seeks a way to reconcile the new view with what he already believes. The average voter listens to the television broadcast of the man for whom he already plans to vote to provide reenforcement for his position. Similarly the consumer watches the commercial for the product that he has just purchased rather than the message of the competition to avoid challenge to his decision.

3. The decoder focuses his attention on messages from the encoder he respects. The teacher, in the traditional, linear student-teacher relationship, has the built-in complementary role of authority, which helps him to gain attention. But, in some traditional classrooms, students are so busy scanning teacher messages for personal approval that there is little content decoded and relatively little interaction with peers.

4. The decoder focuses attention on the easy stimuli. In this, what psychologists call the "minimal principle," the organism tends to accept the simplest description of the information it receives. Given an easy spoken message, the decoder will attend to it better than to one that is for some reason obscured.

Since our perception is a unit of experience that combines into a new organization of present and past subsystems, it is very difficult to predict the effect(s) of any message. Studies show that young people are open to the perception of messages that disagree with their views, but after the junior year in college students have acquired most of the ethical and political views that they will hold twenty years later.[6] The student equipped for modern living is aware of the complexity of perception and readily questions the categories in which he places his sensory impressions.

Although the importance of an understanding of human perception is central to all areas of communication, verbal and nonverbal, this importance is perhaps best illustrated in the students' participation in communication processing.

[6] Mervin B. Friedman, "Studies of College Alumni," in Nevitt Sanford (ed.), *The American College* (New York: Wiley, 1964), pp. 847–886.

PHASE 3

THE PROCESSING:
The Communication-Oriented Classroom

It's All in the Wrong Place

My mind holds this world in the palms of its hands,
and with one single thought I can destroy
or turn it into a Garden of Eden.
I can mold it like clay into any size or shape I want to.
I can open it and explore its inners.
But I am like any man.
. . . . Handicapped.
For this is all in my mind.

J.M., age 17

from *the me nobody knows*

Six

The Components of Speech Communication

In a "life style" devoted to responsible participation in highly complex communication systems, how do we train the human communicators in the classroom workshop designed for life? What communication skills do our students need to live meaningful lives?

THE HUMAN COMPONENT

Most importantly, we must work consistently to understand the communication system in which we are involved; regular and organized evaluation to guard against possible communication breakdown must take place. For the occupants of a classroom this means sharp awareness of the limitations of their communication system, literal understanding of the components of that system, and what can—and must—be expected of these components. Assume that an urban classroom has thirty students, ranging in age from ten to twelve, whose backgrounds might include representative groups from an American urban community: second generation white Greek-American; third generation white conservative Jew of Russian background; fourth generation American black from a ghetto; white Italian-American of orthodox Catholic stock; white Protestant from an affluent fifth generation family, to name several. Possibly one person is designated to guide these thirty human variables. One person facilitates

77

the learning of these varying races, religions, socioeconomic, and educational levels, and, perhaps most important, varying human values and attitudes. This designated facilitator, the teacher, is an additional complex communicator of a more advanced age, more deeply ingrained conscious and unconscious attitudes, and—for better or worse—more advanced, formal education verified, perhaps, by a master's degree.

These thirty-one communicators, then, constitute the human components of a communication system. The primary task within this classroom is to work to achieve an atmosphere devoid of personal threat, which might distort accurate communication. Although we reward a student's traditional accomplishments with percentage or letter grades, rarely do we reward the student's and teacher's endeavors to explore the personalities of fellow students within the classroom. Rarely do we recognize the critical importance of devoting extensive time within a given classroom to the primary research of getting to know each other *in depth* so that whatever verbal and nonverbal communication proceeds between and among the inhabitants of the classroom—the world—can be built on the more solid and meaningful ground of what we *know* about each other—not what we think we know about each other, not what others have told us about each other, not what the conventional labels that we use for each other dupe us into thinking we know about each other. At one given moment within the classroom the immediate communication system may involve a teacher having a conference with a student while the other students listen; the communication system may involve a student dyad while the rest of the class listens and verbally participates periodically or numerous other combinations of communication systems and subsystems.

But whatever the permutations and combinations of thirty-one human beings may be, communication will not take place unless these communicators have shared similar language experiences. Communicators that make contact meaningfully must have covered an area of life space similarly—and when possible—together; the larger this shared space, the more chance for meaningful communication encounters. Wilbur Schramm pictorializes this concept in Figure 6–1.[1]

Shared language experience has at its foundation at least definite denotative meanings. If a class similar to the one described above were to use prescribed reading materials designed for the Midwestern predominantly white, Christian community—like the popular "Dick and Jane" series—there would be little if any life space shared. However, materials drawn

[1] Wilbur Schramm, *The Process and Effects of Mass Communication* (Urbana: University of Illinois Press, 1961), p. 6. Reprinted by permission.

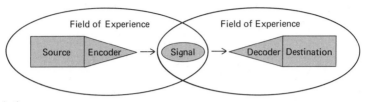

FIG 6–1

from the students' personal experiences, even books written by the students themselves, can provide the opportunity for classroom communicators to read and talk about their own backgrounds. Similarly, activities shared in the community should be shared within the classroom to discover and enlarge the mutual span of life. Ideally, for optimum conditions of communication, participants in a given communication system would share all aspects of their lives. Even then, total communication accuracy could only be approached.

The time in the classroom may only be the beginning of the task of communication; but the important aspect for the teacher to realize is that a group working for precision of communication based on genuine understanding of the humans involved is worth taking beyond the classroom. The classroom devoted to rote memory and graded for success and approval may discourage a communicator's desire to discover *why* human communicators make certain responses. Security for the student, and moreover for the teacher, becomes the mechanical ability to provide the "right answer"—that is, the *expected* answer—in the quickest amount of time. It is as if we were encouraged to behave like machines, because our lives have been made easier by machines. John Holt in *How Children Fail* makes this statement:

> We adults [teachers?] destroy most of the intellectual and creative capacity of children by the things we do to them or make them do. We destroy this capacity above all by making them afraid, afraid of not doing what other people want, of not pleasing, of making mistakes, of failing, of being *wrong*. Thus we make them afraid to gamble, afraid to experiment, afraid to try the difficult and the unknown. Even when we do not create children's fears, when they come to us with fears ready-made and built-in, we use these fears as handles to manipulate them and get them to do what we want. Instead of trying to whittle down their fears, we build them up, often to monstrous size. For we like children who are a little afraid of us, docile, deferential children, though not, of course, if they are so obviously afraid that they threaten our image of ourselves as kind, lovable people whom there is no reason to fear. . . . We destroy the disinterested (I do

not mean *un*interested) love of learning in children, which is so strong when they are small, by encouraging and compelling them to work for petty and contemptible rewards—gold stars, or papers marked 100 and tacked to the wall, of A's on report cards, or honor rolls, or dean's lists of Phi Beta Kappa keys—in short, for the ignoble satisfaction of feeling that they are better than someone else. We encourage them to feel that the end and aim of all they do in school is nothing more than to get a good mark on a test, or to impress someone with what they seem to know. We kill, not only their curiosity, but their feeling that it is a good and admirable thing to be curious, so that by the age of ten most of them will not ask questions, and will show a good deal of scorn for the few who do. . . . We encourage children to act stupidly, not only by scaring and confusing them, but by boring them, by filling up their days with dull, repetitive tasks that make little or no claim on their attention or demands on their intelligence. Our hearts leap for joy at the sight of a roomful of children all slogging away at some imposed task, and we are all the more pleased and satisfied if someone tells us that the children don't really like what they are doing. We tell ourselves that this drudgery, this endless busywork, is good preparation for life. . . . Before long they are deeply settled in a rut of unintelligent behavior from which most of them could not escape even if they wanted to.[2]

The environment required for a communication system to proceed at a responsible level, then, is one that encourages a student to probe, explore, and experiment with *every* aspect of the communication system; and to recognize the infinite complexity of each part of a communication system, of each communicator. In the classroom the student should not have to worry about risking acceptance and rejection by experimenting in what amounts to a human relations laboratory. Whereas the student in his family and various life situations may be involved with *emotionally* motivated input, processing, output, and feedback to gain acceptance and love through learned techniques, in the classroom the student must grow to the security that he is not risking rejection by experimenting, questioning, investigating in depth every aspect of the human communication process. In family and social situations we are too often trained to provide expected responses for approval; we rarely risk disapproval for fear of rejection. Risk in experimentation in the classroom must always be possible and encouraged often. The teacher must motivate and develop in the classroom an atmosphere in which every aspect of the communication system can be explored.

[2] John Holt, *How Children Fail* (New York: Dell, 1964), pp. 167–168, 169–170.

THE DENOTATIVE AND CONNOTATIVE COMPONENTS

Specifically, what must participants in a communication system control at the input stage of communication? What must a student consciously recognize regarding the verbal code (the words) as the encoding (the literal putting of a thought into words) occurs. The student must understand that words, spoken and written, carry both denotative (literal, nonpersonal) meanings as well as connotative (abstract, highly personal) meanings. Even the seemingly most denotative verbal code may provoke in the receiver of the message, the decoder, a highly connotative, personal response.

Words such as "house" and "rooms" in a student's utterance, "The house I live in has four rooms," may appear relatively safe at the denotative level; but a student communicator who is an only child living with his mother and father in this space may decode the message differently from a student who is one of five children living with bickering parents in a similar space. Certainly the classroom communicators, with the teacher as facilitator, cannot be expected to stop before each utterance to explore the multiple possibilities of interpretation; likewise, each message, once processed, cannot be analyzed in detail by thirty decoders in our hypothetical classroom. But we can as communicators in a controlled learning environment begin early in our education to recognize our responsibilities and regularly take time to analyze, individually and as a group, the encoding, processing, and decoding elements.

We know that no matter how hard a class has worked to understand fully all possible aspects of the human communicators within the communication system, it is never entirely possible to assure absolute meaning at a denotative level. The class must know this, and knowing this, work to accomplish the impossible. This attempt must be an on-going process. A communicator in the classroom, whether a student or a teacher, must always be willing to ask, "What do you mean?" Each participant in the communication systems and subsystems of that classroom must willingly clarify and amplify the message, especially, when communication becomes muddled. Furthermore, when words are explored in the learning laboratory to discover how connotative associations might motivate creativity in an unthreatening environment, the results may provide students with truly enlightening insights for enlarging their mutual life space. In *Creative Power* Hughes Mearns argues for imaginative use of communication systems approach to classroom group procedure; he reminds us what school "life" too often is:

> One learns early in life that expressing of one's unique individuality does not pay. The sure way to become disliked is to express one's real self.

Disliked? Hated, rather. If one disbelieves, an easy proof is near; for one may at any time, with a little practice, reach into the sure current that runs quietly within us, wherein flows our honest reactions to the life about us. The truth is always there, the truth as we see it, contradicting all the polite agreements that are voluble on the surface of daily living. Reach within and pluck it out for a single day and see what the world will do to you! Now it is the cultivating of this individual sense for the truth which is the beginning of wisdom, even though one declines to be so impolitic as to try it on a conventional world; but to wall it up so that it is beyond any possible reach, until, indeed, the possessor is finally unaware of its existence, that is the Great Stupidity. It is those who thus immure their birthright, however, who teach the young that its naive self-expression is an unholy thing.[3]

Mearns' statement may be illustrated by the following three creative expressions by a class of children working on self-discovery to aid these human communicators. In response to the words "house," "rooms," and "doors" the following statements of personal associations—connotations— were achieved. The ages of the writers are indicated:

The Memory-Filled House

Along the long, dark hallway,
Up the memory-filled stairs,
Walking down the back way,
In the bare kitchen, with a harshness in the air,
In the dining room, no table or chair,
On the sideboard, no apple, orange, or pear,
In Grandma's room, no pictures on the wall,
Again, down the long, dark hall.
                                        —10 years old[4]

Oh, Joyous House

When I walk home from school,
I see many houses
Many houses down many streets.
They are warm, comfortable houses

[3] Hughes Mearns, *Creative Power: The Education of Youth in the Creative Arts* (New York: Dover Publications, Inc., 1958), p. 25.

[4] Richard Lewis, *Miracles* (New York: Simon and Schuster, 1966), p. 177. Reprinted by permission.

But other people's houses
I pass without much notice.

Then as I walk farther, farther
I see a house, the house.
It springs up with a jerk
That speeds my pace; I lurch forward.
Longing makes me happy, I bubble inside.
It's my house.

—12 years old[5]

The Doors

The doors in my house
Are used every day
For closing rooms
And locking children away.

—10 years old[6]

DENOTATIVE-CONNOTATIVE AMBIGUITIES

The following transcript illustrates various communication difficulties that must be recognized and handled. This dialogue—a discussion that took place in an upstate New York high school after the students had listened to a speech on clothing styles—is a collective adaptation from many classes and is used here for illustrative purposes:

Miss Nichols: What problem do we have currently today on fashions? What's—you know—what's the problem or what are the problems?
Bob: Sitting down.
Miss Nichols: (*with surprise in voice*) Sitting down is a problem—with a mini skirt—good. What other problems?
Bob: Bending over.
Miss Nichols: Bending over— What else?
Bob: Prejudice.
Miss Nichols: Prejudice— What do you mean? Fads?
Bob: About the boys have feminine clothes, which isn't true.
Miss Nichols: All the boys have feminine clothes, which isn't true. Lenore.
Lenore: No—some people can't wear them.

[5] *Ibid.*, p. 152.
[6] *Ibid.*, p. 166.

Miss Nichols: Wear what?
Lenore: Those fad men's fashions—or, like mini skirts on fat people. They look stupid.
Ray: Yeah, pitiful.
Hank: May I say something, Miss Nichols?
Miss Nichols: After Lenore.
Lenore: I finished.
Miss Nichols: Have you finished? Can you go further with that? With what you started?
Lenore: Well, you shouldn't wear them if you are not made to wear them. You should wear things for yourself and not just because they are a fad.
Miss Nichols: Just because they are a fad. O.K. Hank.
Hank: Well, if a girl's walking down the street and she has a mini skirt on and some boy whistles to her, she shouldn't get mad cause it's her own fault.
Ray: Yeah.
Hank: I mean she's wearing that just to show off.
Ray: Yeah, that's right.
Miss Nichols: She's wearing it just to show off. Do you agree girls?
Girls: No.
Hank: If some boy whistles at her—or makes fun—or laughs at her—it's her own fault. She shouldn't turn around and slap him or something.
Ray: That's right. That's right. That's why she's doing it.

To begin with, the teacher's question is vague and confusing. "Fashions" presumably means styles of clothing worn by the students; the immediate student reactions make it clear that fashions *in clothing* is the teacher's intended topic. The word "problem," judging from the immediate response by Bob, is not meaningful. Student decoding depends on immediate, personal interpretation of what constitutes a literal "problem." Although Bob's response is reasonable in terms of the phrasing of the question, the teacher responds "with surprise in voice" but, according to the verbal code she uses, fails to realize that her meaning for "problem" is still misunderstood. "Bending over" is cited by Bob as another "problem." In the classroom oriented for precision of communication not only would the teacher aim to clarify her own thinking with a more precise control of language, but the student would feel the immediate responsibility to everyone involved in the communication system—here an entire class and a teacher engaged in general discussion on one topic—to question the teacher's imprecision of language. The students might ask: Do you mean clothing fashions? hair fashions? fashionable behavior? By "we" do you mean men and women? students? children being supported by parents?

And with the word "problems" should we consider the appropriateness of the clothing to the event? what clothes we should wear to school? the "problems" of fit and movement? Or, perhaps, should we consider the more inclusive "problem": Do our parents understand how our generation has been expressing itself through the clothes teen-agers wear today, in school and out? Although the transcript used here doesn't include the teacher's clarification of what she intended for discussion, the last hypothetical question is what the teacher originally intended. The class never reached this aspect of the topic. Before the students and teacher allowed the discussion to progress, however aimlessly, the original question of the teacher should have been sufficiently clarified to provide a reasonable basis for denotative understanding and meaningful progress.

But the confusion in the classroom discussion may illustrate more potentially dangerous areas. After Bob names some of the literal problems the female might face in wearing a very short skirt, he suggests the more abstract problem of "prejudice." Although the teacher quickly asks, "What do you mean?" the discussion proceeds without a definite clarification of what Bob does, in fact, mean by the word "prejudice." Although the topic of clothing may be of real concern to the class, the use of the word "prejudice" in this context probably would not provoke the connotative value it might have in the context of, say, a racial or religious discussion. Yet perhaps for just this reason, the use of the word should have been explored and defined further. At the moment the word was used might the teacher or a concerned member of the class have asked other class members for a definition of "prejudice"? Might it have been useful, in an environment established as a communication system in which we accepted such a technique, for a teacher to have turned to a black student and a Jewish student—and a particularly short or tall student—and other students representing minorities to ask for word associations that spring to mind spontaneously upon hearing the word "prejudice"? Or, might the teacher, at the moment Bob used the word, have told each member of the class to take paper and pencil and write a brief definition of the word and then give each member of the class an opportunity to read his definition aloud? Similarities and differences in definitions would no doubt occur. The reasons for their existence might be probed as a way of underscoring how meanings emerge. After all, the discussion of teen-age fashions and the so-called generation gap in a classroom geared to achieving efficient communication systems would be used less for the factual, informational aspects and more for the exploration of how meaning is achieved in a group.

But, further, might the students have investigated *why* Bob seemed spontaneously to choose the word "prejudice"? Has he misused an emotionally charged word? If so, in more crucial discussions of more critical import, such as race relations, would he glibly employ a word like "prejudice" due to his denotative inaccuracy, thereby possibly getting himself into trouble through connotative decodings in the system? Did he, indeed, mean "prejudice" in this discussion? Or did he, perhaps, mean "misinformation"? "ignorance"? "narrow-mindedness"? If any students in the classroom, as receivers of Bob's utterance had been victims of personal "prejudice," Bob may have provoked unexpected, nonverbalized reactions that may promote communication difficulties later. Certainly, it is more important for Bob to realize the multiple meanings he may have provoked in the decoders with "prejudice" than for the teacher to go on to Lenore for further comments of questionable pertinence. In a communication-oriented classroom system, student and teacher would be trained to know the importance of clarifying such a culturally loaded word as "prejudice."

This basic communication principal of pursuing denotative and connotative meaning between and among communicators, encoders and decoders, is further illustrated in the following excerpt from a kindergarten interaction:

Miss Dully:	What did you bring back from our walk on the beach?
David:	I found a starfish.
Miss Dully:	Oh, that's interesting. . . . What does a starfish look like?
Patty:	It looks like a key.
Miss Dully:	It looks like a key?
Patty:	A little key.
Miss Dully:	(after a momentary pause) What is it? Is it a bird?
Ellen:	No, it's not a bird.
Raymond:	(laughing) It's a fish!
Miss Dully:	Good Raymond and where do fish live?
Several voices in unison:	In the water!

When the kindergarteners are examining David's starfish with exuberance, the teacher attempts to steer the discussion to an organized analysis with the question "What is a starfish?" Patty responds, "It looks like a key." Caught off guard by the response, the teacher returns Patty's message as a question: "It looks like a key?" Patty elaborates the description, "A little key." The teacher, insistent upon pursuing her own demands that the children identify the object as a fish that lives in water, continues with, "What is it? Is it a bird?" From this point on, Patty's identification of the starfish with a key is lost, to all intents and purposes, to history. Rather than pursue the child's vocabulary choice to attempt to discover why Patty identifies this strange pointed object with a key, Patty's imaginative utterance is discarded. The class, the members of this *beginning,* formative, but still highly complex communication system, needs to exercise immediately the nature of Patty's utterance. Furthermore, what do the decoders of this message, the other children in the class, think Patty means by the word "key" as a description of the starfish? By proceeding to safer grounds of identification, is the teacher discouraging Patty and the other human variables in the room from future spontaneity? This is difficult if, at all, possible to judge. But if "key" is a random, mistaken association, the communicators within the kindergarten system should have been encouraged to discover the inaccuracy. The teacher as facilitator in the communication systems of the classroom must be aware of such possibilities; otherwise he or she has no defensible right to be there. Is the kindergarten teacher primarily teaching the students to identify a starfish? Or is the teacher using the starfish as an immediate, experiential illustration of how minds work to identify and label aspects of our environment, to attach labels that depend for meaning on the previous experiences—pertinent or otherwise—that automatically influence the encoder in new situations?

COMMUNICATION BREAKDOWN

The vital need to establish an environment of experience and inquiry in the classroom throughout a communicator's continuing education is perhaps more dramatically illustrated by an incident in 1969 on the campus of Wesleyan University, a traditionally esteemed, liberal American university. The university, like many others throughout the country, was disrupted by student and faculty confrontations regarding the rights of blacks on a predominantly white campus. Numerous incidents threatened to erupt into violence. The *New York Times Magazine* reported the following:

> The story . . . began early this fall with a rash of burglaries in the dormitories. White students suspected three or four blacks who had been seen frequently wandering through the corridors of several dorms. One night a white student, hearing a knock at his door, and suspecting larcenous intentions, decided not to answer. The door opened and two blacks appeared. "Sorry," one of them said, "we thought this was the bathroom."
>
> The white student made a sarcastic remark about the difficulties of finding clearly-labeled bathroom doors. More words led to a fight with one of the black students, during which the other black, George Walker, pulled a knife—not to attack, he said later, but to prevent other whites

who had rushed to the scene from interceding. It turned out that Walker was one of the "San Francisco Five"—alleged Black Panthers from Wesleyan whom San Francisco police had arrested last spring and charged with illegal possession of weapons.

Thirteen days after the fight, Wesleyan's five-man Student Judiciary Board (S. J. B.—four whites, one black) put Walker and his friend on strict disciplinary probation, meaning that any further trouble would lead to automatic expulsion. At the same time S.J.B. issued an "official warning" to the white student, noting that his language may have been belligerent.

The decision triggered the next disaster. On Nov. 4, Jonathan Berb, a white senior from New Jersey, wrote a fiery letter to the Argus in which he called the S. J. B. ruling on the white student "just incredible" and called Walker "a common criminal" and "a punk." *In black argot, and unknown to Berg, "punk" means homosexual.* That night about a dozen blacks went to Berg's room and threatened him with physical harm if he did not retract the statement. The next night Walker paid another call on Berg, found him taking a shower, and beat him up. . . .[7]

Central issues in the reported event, if the language and the attitude of the *New York Times* article writer are to be trusted, occurred because decoders drew conclusions or made decisions from emotionally loaded messages received under extreme personal stress. The writer indicates that "a sarcastic remark" was made, and "more words led to a fight"; in the fight the nonverbal behavior of pulling a knife was explained later as a preventive device, but during the fight surely the nonverbal statement communicated the threat of a lethal weapon. Later in the report, the writer accurately or inaccurately equates the white student's "sarcastic remark" with the Student Judiciary Board's warning to the white student, "noting that his language may have been belligerent." Not only were there clearly communication problems of those participants in the Wesleyan system, but the reporter of that system's activities may also carry distortion for the reader of the article. Various aspects of this incident demonstrate communication breakdowns; many of these breakdowns may find their mutual source in the virtual noncommunication on an experiential level between black and white in America for hundreds of years. But the critical point here is the use of the word "punk," which triggered violence; a highly specialized usage of an already colloquial, connotative word uttered under circumstances of crisis produced unexpected, destructive results. It would be naïve—absurd!—to suggest that

[7] Richard J. Margolis, "The Two Nations at Wesleyan University," *The New York Times Magazine,* January 18, 1970, p. 62.

the blacks and whites involved might have probed meaning of the word "punk" before taking action. What is quite real, however, is the evidence that decades of education devoted to ignoring meaning at the denotative level have led to literal racial revolution; that a nation that accepted the phrase "free the slaves" in 1863 took one hundred years to investigate the practical meaning and application of that phrase.

Similarly, Ralph Ellison, in 1947, won prizes for his book *The Invisible Man;* it sold thousands of copies. A predominantly white public read the book's first line: "I am an invisible man."[8] The author devoted hundreds of pages to explaining the "invisibility" of a black human being. But not until twenty years later, with the rise of "black power," the crisis in urban schools, and the active and often destructive racial demonstrations, did we begin to see that "invisible" man. It is foolhardy to suggest that we can undo the communication roadblocks to the past; but it is crucial for us to implement more accurate, shared communication in the present and future. If the classroom as a communication laboratory explores the lives of each of the communicators and provides the students with a realization that his personal experience is not the only possible experience, if the meaning of the encoder's message is approached with at least the realization that a particular life experience influences that message, at least the human communicator has a chance of understanding his fellow-man. You must understand that my choice of verbal and nonverbal messages depends on my life experience, on my perceptions. If you don't recognize and analyze my life and how I communicate it in relation to your life, and how I interpret your life, we will inevitably remain "invisible" to each other.

Is it unreasonable to ask whether the human black and white variables at Wesleyan communicating at a time of extreme personal and public crisis had had any training in the complexities of human communication systems? And what would happen if, someday, one of these students had to make that ultimate, "hot line" decision? It is entirely reasonable for a teacher to consider the classroom student communicators as potential presidents, vice-presidents, secretaries of states, generals in strategic command posts. The training a student needs in accurate communication should serve him in *any* responsible position, from the most personal to the most public. Lyndon Johnson made this point eminently clear after his tenure as President when he stated:

And I concluded that [Mrs. Johnson] was wrong, that we should not undertake another term as President because of the divisiveness that I

---

[8] Ralph Ellison, *The Invisible Man* (New York: Signet Books, 1952), p. 7.

could see ahead, because of the feeling of the Negro militants that was then asserting itself, because of the reaction of the South, and the attitude of the people of the North toward the South and vice versa, and the reaction of the press media and how they reacted to things I said and did—my manner, my style, and how I—from my viewpoint, how they twisted and imagined and built and magnified things that I didn't think were true at all. I never thought it was the President's credibility gap, I thought it was their credibility gap. But they owned the papers and the networks; I didn't. And they come out every day. And they could talk about my credibility, but there wasn't much I could do about their credibility.[9]

In view of the Wesleyan black-white confrontation consider the following transcript of a class discussion in a primary school in New York City:

Teacher (*to the class*):   Did you ever hear the poem called "Frosting"?[10]
(*She reads.*)
                Freedom is just frosting from somebody else's cake
                And so it must be until we learn to bake.
What does that mean? Freedom is just frosting from somebody else's cake. What does it mean?

Child: It means freedom is like sugar.

Teacher: But why is it on somebody else's cake?

Child: Somebody is gonna give it to us?

Teacher: Why, do you think? Why is it on somebody else's cake?

Child: Because we don't have freedom right now, and it's like a luxury he saw somebody else have.

Teacher: That's very good.

Child: Because we are black people.

Teacher: Why? What about cake? Let's talk about cake.

Child: He's talking about—um—he's putting the freedom on their cake because he didn't have his freedom.

Teacher: He didn't have his freedom. (*Turning to another student*) What do you think?

Child: Because he . . . I say the same thing.

Teacher (*to another student*):   You say the same thing?

Child: Until you learn how to bake, half of you won't have any freedom.

Child: That's what he's saying—but he really means that until he learns how to get his own freedom, it'll just be something he looks at that other people have.

[9] Lyndon B. Johnson, "Why I Chose Not to Run," Transcript of CBS News Special as broadcast over the CBS Television Network, December 27, 1969, p. 4.
[10] Langston Hughes, *The Panther and the Lash* (New York: Knopf, 1969), p. 84. Reprinted by permission. Also reprinted by permission of Harold Ober Associates.

In this dialogue the teacher is attempting to guide youngsters to an understanding of "freedom," or so it would seem. But she begins with a questionable metaphor from a poem and insists upon pursuing that metaphor when the students keep trying to solidify the discussion with personal identifications like "Because we are black people." To this child the teacher says, "Let's talk about cake." To confront a young mind with the term "freedom" and to assume that everyone agrees on a definition of this dangerously abstract word is to capitulate immediately to an educational concept founded on meaningless generalizations. The students in this class are trying to tell the teacher that they don't have this amorphous "thing" glibly called "freedom" because they are black and a white community doesn't even recognize their existence; that "freedom" is not a matter of cake or icing or any such abstraction; that to mouth the standard, accepted, grammar school concept of "we must earn the right to be free" is an exercise in avoidance. What defense could be made of employing and pursuing this cliché for its own sake in a communication system attempting to establish clear, honest lines of communication between and among minority groups oppressed for centuries and finally taking a stand for human survival? Does the teacher, the leader in this sensitive communications laboratory,—whatever we think of her judgment regarding the use of this particular metaphor—believe that cake and frosting are more meaningful to children than their own terminology of black and white? She is leading them into abstraction, into imprecision. She is also playing it safe. In her attempt to teach the children to "think"—which she would probably list as her "goal" or "aim" in this "lesson"—she is encouraging the acceptance of pat generalities like "freedom." Where is the precision? Where is the thinking? Where is the confrontation with life? If riots erupted in the halls of this particular school at this moment, would the teacher rely on metaphors of cake and icing with her classes in attempting penetrating discussion of the school's problems? Perhaps the motives of the teacher—and her methods courses, which may have led her into these avenues of avoidance—were well-intended. But this is no excuse for classrooms that train for confusion, for obfuscation based on traditionally accepted generalizations.

But what other methodology might the teacher have employed? Might she have started with the unfinished sentence, "When I am free, I am . . ." and allowed each student to provide a suggestion and then explore the nature of the choices, the possible groupings or the responses, the reasons for contrast, the basis for choice? No child is too young to discover why he associates "free" with a particular personal activity, with a particular person. If a student suggests an abstraction, such as "When I am free, I am an American," such a generality should be pursued;

furthermore, the students should be encouraged to pursue and complete their ideas. It is easy, and a dangerous "cop out," for a student at any age to respond, "I say the same thing," without an attempt on the part of fellow students and teacher, all participators in the active communication system at work, to seek amplification of the agreement. Easy agreement may breed unnecessary passivity; human passivity may impede active, open channels of communication.

APPROPRIATE LANGUAGE BEHAVIOR

Assuming, then, that this basic cognitive process is regularly pursued with oral language in the classroom, how can the human communicator grow to have a reasonable, sensible control over the *spoken quantity of the message,* which constitutes the major element of input into the communication system? What must a student practice consciously to assure accurate production of the spoken words and the ordered pattern of these words into varying units to say what he means? There is a real danger of communication breakdown in discussing literal control of the spoken message. Specifically: Is there anything we can still label "standard spoken American English"?

Teachers today must realize that a prescriptive approach to the teaching and using of voice and diction for the sake of some nebulous standard or "class" association may not only be ignorant of language dynamics but downright dangerous. This is not to say that a student should not be trained to achieve clarity of meaning through accurate use of the structure of English, the vocabulary available, and those sound segments that ensure input and processing that provide the decoder with intended meaning. But the teacher must recognize and deal with the background that has produced those sounds; a student's idiolect—his distinguishing and unique speech—is generally an accurate reflection of major aspects of that student's life experience. The teacher as facilitator must never make a value judgment regarding any student's "correctness" of idiolect.

Student communicators must also be trained in this area, as in all learning, to avoid value judgments based on generalized cultural behavior, which is easily misunderstood. The New Yorker who articulates certain consonants in a manner different from that of a Chicagoan is rarely "better" or "worse" than this other person; the reason for the difference is simply that personal life experiences have strongly influenced each encoder's message. True, this influence may consciously or unconsciously affect the decoding by those decoders who may articulate certain sounds differently from the encoder. The student must understand that his language, verbal and nonverbal, may vary considerably from one situation to another; that a communicator's language probably needs to become more flexible, more disciplined, and more adaptable as education and mobility increase. Mary Smith, a high school student in southwest Chicago, Illinois, who uses a dialectal speech pattern including the vowel pronunciation heard in her region may train to be a high school English teacher. If she becomes a teacher, Mary must decide whether her personal speech habits, as she now controls them, reflect accurate meaning when applied to the demands of language and literature teaching; furthermore, Mary must decide how much mobility she wants as a teacher. If she decides to teach outside of Chicago, will her idiolect, which she uses without causing a communication systems breakdown in southwest Chicago schools, communicate similar meanings in northern California? in New York? in Florida? Indeed, are there variations of the sounds Mary already uses that she should recognize and practice *if* she wants mobility as a teacher?

And if Mary plans instead to marry and settle in southwest Chicago and pursue a career as a secretary, will she have any need for a "standard" beyond the standards established by her geographical region? If teachers are to facilitate learning through mutual understanding, the sonic elements in message processing must be recognized for what they are and to the extent that they can be used. The student who enrolls in a college course entitled "Speech for the Radio Newscaster" expects training that will qualify him for a job that may take his speech communication habits to all parts of the world. Presumably his oral American English must be understood by anyone who speaks the language, whatever the decoder's particular dialectal pattern might be. This student of broadcasting must be willing to train his speech for his job. If the student, for whatever linguistic reason, omits final sounds in words and produces vowels that identify him regionally, he must work for control or settle for a job on a local station with a limited audience. But if the student decides to learn new sounds for new situations, we all must understand, as human communicators, that the student may choose to use his original idiolect to communicate in all situations outside the broadcasting environment. But this is the communicator's decision. The child in a ghetto elementary school must not learn that his speech patterns, and by inference those of his home and environment, are "bad" or even reflect "ignorance"—or, too often, "stupidity." Such an approach can only result in further ignorance and the kind of hostility that impedes communication.

On the other hand, what the student does need to know, from elementary through graduate school, is the degree of oral clarity he is achieving in a given communication system and how he might, if he chooses, control that clarity appropriately to the message. Although "appropriate" has been stressed for years in clarifying elements of speech to distill intended meaning, the word has been readily and regularly distorted to mean that one standard is appropriate to all situations. Phoney sounds and artificial posing have passed too often for precise communication. In our context "appropriate" must be understood as the language behavior, verbal and nonverbal, that may achieve optimum communication of intended meaning within a given situation. The same communicator, the human variable, may find his language at home markedly different in sound and structure from the language used on the bus ride to school; and his "bus language" with friends may vary markedly from his language with the same friends during a small group discussion an hour later in his English class on the question, "Do television commercials influence our verbal and nonverbal language in America today?" Each situation may demand changes in processing into oral messages to achieve accurate meaning. And all may be appropriate.

THE COMPONENTS OF SPEECH

Assuming that all participants in a communication system genuinely understand the descriptive, as opposed to the prescriptive, nature of language learning and assuming that these participants desire to control the oral elements in encoding and processing the message, certain recommendations may be useful.

Vocal information can be isolated into five components of the oral message: (1) volume (intensity), (2) rate, (3) pitch, (4) vocal quality, (5) articulation and pronunciation. The meaning of a spoken communication is carried by the vocal delivery comprised of these five components of speech; a personal attitude, an individual point of view, is communicated to a listener immediately upon the speaker's particular oral treatment of the message. Denotative and connotative meaning of the message may vary in as many ways as there are available combinations of these components.

Let us clarify the five components specifically: Volume refers to the degree of loudness of a sound, the audibility; rate refers to speed, how fast or slow the message is uttered; pitch refers to how high or low a sound is delivered, as on a musical scale; vocal quality refers to the texture of the voice, such as harsh, strident, mellow; articulation refers to the manner in which each individual sound, each vowel or consonant in English, for example, is produced by the organs of speech, and pronunciation refers to the combinations of these sounds into utterances called words, our verbal code. When the communicator begins to encode, as oral input proceeds, the communicator must realize that the five elements of speech are constantly working at some level of meaning and are crucial to the accuracy, not only of the encoding, but of the immediate processing and reception of the message; feedback—whether positive or negative—may be a direct result of the encoder's skill in appropriately controlling the components of speech.

It is vital that the teacher realize that the phrase "components of speech" literally refers to the oral, the spoken, process of human communication. As obvious as this may seem, it is necessary, since we have other similar phrases, glibly used by teacher and student alike, that purport to refer to speech but are traditionally restricted to written not oral communication. Two such phrases are "parts of speech" and "figures of speech." Have you, as teacher or student, ever considered individually or in a group why these grammatic labels are "parts of *speech*"? Such automatic labels as noun, pronoun, adjective, and adverb are used to identify the "parts" of written sentences. What have these labels to do with speech, with *oral and aural* communication? Indeed, as taught and challenged by techniques of modern linguistics theory, what basis in fact do these labels rightly have in the English language? If these labels are used abundantly in class, are students unconsciously identifying as speech aspects of written language that are not, literally, *parts* of speech? The spoken act of spoken processing is rarely if ever considered; and what of "figures of speech"? This phrase is generally a convenient handle used in traditional literature discussions for analyzing imaginative writing techniques, techniques labeled as simile, metaphor, personification, and so on. But the elements of speech, the components pertinent to speaking and hearing, are rarely included in discussion. It is the *written* representation that is considered as a "figure of speech." What qualifies these techniques as "speech"? What purpose is this facile labeling serving for the student in need of communication skills? The "components of speech," however, are integral, required aspects of the oral communication process: A human verbal spoken utterance automatically exists at a certain measurable loudness level, spoken at a measurable speed at a measurable pitch level with a characteristic textural quality to the sound; furthermore, the clarity of meaningful language sounds and words can be analyzed. The "elements of speech" are actually components of the message spoken and heard.

CONTROLLING THE COMPONENTS OF SPEECH

In the communication laboratory called the classroom, then, the student must be keenly aware of the way alteration of any or/and all the elements of speech immediately affects all connotative levels of meaning. Teachers can experiment with a portion of the conversation quoted earlier from man's first landing on the moon. The Houston voice said, in part: "You've a bunch of guys about to turn blue. We're breathing again. Thanks a lot." Let a student encode "Thanks a lot" by consciously varying the components of speech of the input. As the message is processed, suggest that the decoders note in writing what is communicated about the person who is speaking, what *attitude* is projected in each vocal treatment of the excerpt. Is the communication important? Is the encoder, as represented by his message, concerned about the decoder and an accurate reception of the message? What elements of feedback does the encoder perceive as the vocal treatment of the excerpt changes? Is the decoder smiling? laughing? grimacing? interrupting? yawning? obviously paying attention? obviously paying little if any attention? The human variable providing the input should seek as many varieties of delivery of the message as possible: Begin simply, speak the message very slowly, loudly, at a comfortably low pitch with "directness" of voice, making sure all appropriate vowel and consonant sounds are clear and words are accurately pronounced; make a straightforward delivery as denotative as possible. Try the message a second time in an attempt to change only *one* component of speech; for example, try to speak the message very rapidly but maintain the other elements at the original delivery level. What change in attitude, in point of view, of the decoder occurs? Now try marked contrast in all the components of delivery, perhaps speaking at a moderate rate in a high-pitched whisper with omission or slurring of some sounds. Perhaps more than one student can participate as an experimenting encoder. After a sizable number of examples have been tried, have the decoders read their notations; help the students discover how change in vocal treatment of the components of speech changed the processing of the communication and affected the decoder. Let the human variables (the students) in the established communication system (the classroom) analyze the varying attitudes decoded. Similarly, the encoder should analyze the manner in which his message obviously changed and how feedback from his listeners changed. Continue the experiment with "We're breathing again" and other messages of increasing structural complexity. For the human being in firm control of his components of speech—his processing apparatus for accurate remittance of sorted data—this will be an illuminating exercise in clarification.

A communicator who recognizes the importance of control of the specific components of his spoken message may exercise his conscious control as specific needs arise; varying needs require varying means of solution in oral communication. But the oral communicator must know whether his oral behavior at a given time is the behavior he intends for solving that particular problem. The situational pressures and other factors may help determine his response as a communicator.

PROBLEM-SOLVING IN THE SMALL GROUP STRUCTURE

In the communication laboratory where the student experiments with behavior to build toward a life space that may provide mutuality of experience with fellow communicators, the teacher as facilitator may, for example, provide the class with problems to be explored for solution through small group structure. If the facilitator in the classroom—and this may be any classroom, at any age or intellectual level, in any of the conventional disciplines—poses a question that can be divided into possible areas of exploration, individual communicators may be pressed into service to communicate orally in many ways. For example, after considering the various topics immediately and mutually pertinent to the lives of the communicators in the communication system (for instance: How does the physical structure of the school limit our learning? Do particular family pressures for success help or hinder our learning in school? What should a student expect from a teacher? Can urban man restore his polluted environment for healthful living?), the class decides on the last subject. The class of thirty divides into five groups, each containing six students. The overall question has been subdivided accordingly, and each group must provide a five-minute spoken factual report in a few days. Within this group structure the individual student may face vocal responsibilities in the roles he assumes. If a particular small group is dealing with the aspect "Does local industry contribute substantially to water pollution in our city through its methods of garbage disposal?" the group may proceed to explore its question in "Ideal Solution Form."[11] That is, the participants in the group consider the following questions to help solve their aspect of the problem: Are we all agreed on the nature of the problem? What would be the ideal solution from the point of view of all parties involved in the problem? What conditions within the problem could be changed so that the ideal solution might be achieved? Of the

[11] Carl E. Larson, "Forms of Analysis and Small Group Problem Solving," *Speech Monographs,* November 1969, p. 453.

solutions available to us which one best approximates the ideal solution? These questions immediately force the communicators into oral participation at some level.

The first question, involving agreement on the nature of the problem, at least requires an oral response, detailed to some degree, which makes certain definite demands on the communicator employing his five components of speech in relating a message clearly, however informally, within the group. The response may be impromptu, based on the speaker's selected experiences, spontaneously organized, and concisely presented. Although the response may be informal, there are definite requirements regarding the communicator's use of volume, rate, pitch, quality, and articulation and pronunciation. Since the group is working toward a factual report, an essentially denotative message, the encoder as well as the decoder must be alert to the appropriate vocal processing, which, for this assignment, must avoid vocal treatment that may suggest personal viewpoint (the projection of *attitude* through vocal delivery).

The group's second question, "What would be the ideal solution from the point of view of all parties involved in the problem?" might demand research of both primary and secondary types. The communicator might need to conduct personal interviews with industrial experts in the city as well as with citizens living in immediate proximity to an industry's waste disposal plants; the researcher might use company reports and newspaper articles containing news items as well as editorials. Whatever the biased nature of the material researched, the student would be required to provide an unbiased vocal summary of sources to the small group for evaluation and possible use.

The third question, "What conditions within the problem could be changed so that the ideal solution might be achieved?" requires group evaluation of the previous suggestions and individual recommendations based on research from each group member. Again, oral delivery of organized thought based on the information collected would be the technique leading to group decision. The communicator must be able to meet the vocal demands of the situation.

The group's final question, "Of the solutions available to us which one best approximates the ideal solution?" should continue to demonstrate the participating communicator's need to state his point of view clearly and to understand whether or not his particular oral message is being encoded, processed, and decoded with appropriate skill. Certainly, as each communicator assumes a role in the group's development, the vocal demands will vary. Feedback within the group will be a strong factor. Ideally, each participant would contribute on an equal basis, and no one person would present the report to the other groups; rather each group member would provide a small spoken contribution to the class as part of his group's findings. But the leader who might emerge to present his group's report should understand how his speech components are the backbone in communicating orally the entire group's factual findings and conclusions; that sound thinking based on adequate research of designated topic area intelligently organized within a given time limit for a particular audience rely for dependable decoding upon the accurate encoding and processing of the spoken message.

Here small groups are working toward factual presentation; denotation is the key to meaning for the group participants in their responsibility to the class as a large communication system. If the oral reporters of each of the five groups then organize into another group and, in this regrouping, decide to try to persuade the class to take definite action to alleviate industrial pollution problems in their city, the goal would change, but the intellectual and vocal responsibilities of the participants would be the same or even more complex. Because persuasion becomes the aim, the group would have to employ substantial research, meaningful organization in relation to time available, and audience analysis. But skillful control in presenting the spoken message becomes even more essential: The voice, in all its components, must support—perhaps convey—the burden of the speaker's commitment to the ideas. Furthermore, it is likely that the student, having moved from participation in one of the five small groups, to individual representative of that group, to member of a specialized group with a specialized purpose, now must act as class representative to convey the point of view for the entire communications system of his classroom to a school assembly, a student organization participating in urban planning or similar groups. Indeed, any of the students should feel a responsibility to report the class progress and discussions to his own family. Whatever the role in whatever group providing and solving whatever needs, the human communicator must apply his vocal skills to serve his ideas. A human being may participate in a group system that has no distinct pattern for problem solving; work begins randomly and tries to find a form. Here the control of the spoken message may be more difficult and more crucial because of the communication breakdowns that might occur through lack of organization. Or the small group structure may strive to clarify one definite question and possible subquestions that require responses. A more traditional small group form that attempts to solve problems through reflective thinking might pose the following questions: "What are the limits and specific nature of the problem? What are the causes and consequences of the problem? What things must an acceptable solution to the problem accomplish? What solutions are available to us? What is the best solution?"[12] These questions provide a stricter structure and perhaps require less possible applied imagination in problem solving. But the spoken message that must be part of the group behavior from the very outset of the group activity requires a constant concern and evaluation of the spoken message's clarity and appropriateness.

Small group activity provides the participating student communicator with the experience of discovering solutions for himself. The sharing of responsibility, the growth of the mutuality of life space, is vigorously exercised. Likewise, the necessity to control the spoken message for appropriate clarity during times of verbalization is discovered. Certainly a class evaluation of the small group experiences regarding the topic "Can urban man restore his polluted environment for healthful living?" should include the effectiveness of the spoken message.

The classroom communication system modeled after life may be training human beings who may, in the future, face responsibilities that control the minds and well-being of millions. The communicator in the following speech transcript has devoted his life to perfecting the written message, but on this occasion a relatively brief spoken message encapsulates a lifetime of belief. The oral communicator here planned his input upon formal speaking considerations: the occasion, the audience, the appropriate time allotment for speaking, the ideas he represents and is determined to reconfirm as crucial in logically organized fashion. He employs verbal language illustrative of his art; the processing represents a human being's life style. The decoders at the event provided verbal and nonverbal feedback at the time of oral delivery, but additional feedback and the involvements of new communication systems have developed since this originally oral message was processed in written form for communicators beyond—in time and space—the initial, immediate occasion. As you read the spoken message printed here, consider the possible appropriate demands the material as written would make if processed orally:

> I feel that this award was not made to me as a man, but to my work—a life's work in the agony and sweat of the human spirit, not for glory and least of all for profit, but to create out of the materials of the human spirit something which did not exist before. So this award is only mine in trust. It will be difficult to find a dedication for the money part of it commensurate with the purpose and significance of its origins. But I would like to do the same with the acclaim too, by using this moment as a pinnacle from which I might be listened to by the young men and women

[12] *Ibid.*

already dedicated to the same anguish and travail, among whom is already that one who will some day stand here where I am standing.

Our tragedy today is a general and universal physical fear so long sustained by now that we can even bear it. There are no longer problems of the spirit. There is only the question: When will I be blown up? Because of this, the young man or woman writing today has forgotten the problem of the human heart in conflict with itself which alone can make good writing because only that is worth writing about, worth the agony and the sweat.

He must learn them again. He must teach himself that the basest of all things is to be afraid; and, teaching himself that, forget it forever, leaving no room in his workshop for anything but the old verities and truths of the heart, the old universal truths lacking which any story is ephemeral and doomed—love and honor and pity and pride and compassion and sacrifice. Until he does so, he labors under a curse. He writes not of love but of lust, of defeats in which nobody loses anything of value, of victories without hope and, worst of all, without pity or compassion. His griefs grieve on no universal bones, leaving no scars. He writes not of the heart but of the glands.

Until he relearns these things, he will write as though he stood among and watched the end of man. I decline to accept the end of man. It is easy enough to say that man is immortal simply because he will endure: that when the last ding-dong of doom has clanged and faded from the last worthless rock hanging tideless in the last red and dying evening, that even then there will still be one more sound: that of his puny, inexhaustible voice, still talking. I refuse to accept this. I believe that man will not merely endure: he will prevail. He is immortal, not because he alone among creatures has an inexhaustible voice, but because he has a soul, a spirit capable of compassion and sacrifice and endurance. The poet's, the writer's, duty is to write about these things. It is his privilege to help man endure by lifting his heart, by reminding him of the courage and honor and hope and pride and compassion and pity and sacrifice which have been the glory of his past. The poet's voice need not merely be the record of man, it can be one of the props, the pillars to help him endure and prevail.

William Faulkner *in acceptance of the 1949 Nobel Prize for Literature*[13]

[13] William Faulkner, *The Faulkner Reader* (New York: Random House, 1954).

Integrating the Written Media

In the best classroom environments, in which the spirit of inquiry is shared by students and teachers, the participants as senders and receivers of messages are trained to monitor their communication behavior for analysis and evaluation. The ideas of other human beings outside the classroom may often be pertinent input into the problem solving and decision making inside the classroom system. The written media—newspaper, book, magazine, letter, and various other forms—are employed to clarify, amplify, and illustrate concepts being considered by thinking students striving for accurate meaning. These written forms are often read aloud in class in order to share and discuss the possible contribution of such material, whatever its source or original purpose. It is important, therefore, for the student participating in modern communication systems to be able to read written material aloud with as much concern and controlled accuracy of meaning as he would want for his own spontaneous, firsthand oral communication.

THE ORAL READER AND THE LISTENER

Oral transmission of the written message is too often taken for granted and assumed to be as easily transmitted in meaningful oral interpretation; the oral reader may not realize that the message, so firmly fixed on the printed page in ordered, printed precision, makes sense to the *listener* only to the degree that the reader—the verbal and nonverbal vehicle of meaning—helps the printed message to be communicated. If the listener had the printed matter in hand and eliminated the oral reader, he—the listener—could reread at his leisure for clarification; he could interrupt the written communication—to answer the door, eat a meal, or what have you—and recapture the meaning by merely rereading that which he had interrupted and continuing at a comfortable silent reading rate. Generally, this ability to review, to say, "Stop and repeat that last sentence, please," is unavailable to the listener of an oral reading. The reading, often crucial as an illustration or amplification of complex ideas under discussion, has one chance in a limited amount of pressured time to make its point. The reader, therefore, has a particular responsibility to control and convey the words of an author who is not present to explain or defend himself against the careless tyranny of an unskilled oral interpreter or an inattentive audience.

Clearly, the basic aim of skillful oral interpretation of written matter is the accurate, appropriate transmission of the author's intended meaning. In Chapter 1 in the transcript devoted to a small group discussion of symbolism in the writings of Ernest Hemingway, the teacher concluded the quoted segment with the question to the class, "Must we always consider the intention of the author?" The resounding, unison group response should have been "Yes!"—particularly if the teacher was referring to the challenge of reading Hemingway aloud with precise, controlled meaning. The transmission of meaning as intended by the author must be the conscious responsibility of the oral reader; and the reader must feel as responsible to plumbing the possible ambiguities of a printed selection for a solid basis of meaning; the reader pursues an intelligent, disinterested analysis to provide a basis for communication in the classroom between and among his fellow communicators. The reader as encoder makes decisions about the author's meaning that, with the use of controlled elements of speech, provide input; the decoder(s) must be allowed to decode accurately the processed information of a third party's—the writer's—message without the possible "noise" of the oral reader's personal attitudes and possibly distorting habitual vocal habits. The oral reader's nonverbal participation—eye contact, involved, meaningful gesture, muscle tonus, facial expression—must complement the oral presentation. Indeed, the oral reader is a kind of transparent, disinterested conveyor of information; this conveyor must be disciplined and unselfish enough not to distort the conveyed message.

READING ALOUD: WORKSHOP BEGINNINGS

If *precise meaning* is our ultimate goal, how does the modern communicator in the classroom system work with a written selection? Even if a student is sharing aloud his own, or his fellow students', communication

ideas in written form, what practical communication principles pertain?
To begin, the student, whether working in class or alone, must approach
reading aloud with the same sense of experimentation that he uses for
other pursuits in his human relations laboratory. That is, the reader must
realize initially that rarely if ever is the oral interpreter able to achieve a
controlled, accurate reading of the printed page on one impromptu
encounter. The endeavor should be treated as a workshop, an active,
mutual undertaking involving an author (represented by his written
work) and the oral readers (one or more) in active, concentrated pursuit
of the author's meaning.

Consider the following selection—from the *New York Times*—as one
chosen by an instructor for workshop sessions to help groups in the
class—perhaps an eighth grade—present illustrative written material that
the groups have decided to examine for intergroup discussion (italics
ours):

> The narrow hallway in 102 *Herzl* Street is as dark and *chill* as
> the wintry street outside. Most of the apartments in the building have
> been abandoned and stripped bare by *vandals*. Plaster crumbles at
> the touch and the stairs groan *ominously*. On the third floor of this
> building Mrs. Nancy Dickerson lives with her three children.   5
>
> The landlord has not been seen there since October. The family
> has been without heat and hot water through most of the winter, and
> gets its only warmth by *leaving the blackened gas stove on 24 hours
> a day.*
>
> "I'm praying until the gas bill comes," Mrs. Dickerson said. "We'll   10
> probably have to go without meat for a few days to pay it. The
> *welfare check* won't cover it."
>
> Mrs. Dickerson held her baby, a bright-eyed girl who has been ill
> with *pneumonia*. Another child, in school at the time, needs *ortho-
> pedic* care. All are in constant danger from the cold, from fires, from   15
> falling plaster. . . .
>
> This is life in the Brownsville section of Brooklyn, until about ten
> years ago a largely Jewish, *working class* community. Today it is
> largely Negro and *Puerto Rican,* and largely forgotten.

To facilitate work, perhaps the instructor has duplicated the chosen
selection to provide a manuscript that is clearly typed, at least double
spaced, and has sufficiently wide margins to accommodate individual
student notations to facilitate oral delivery. If possible, the duplicated
manuscript is distributed the day before it is shared in class to provide
class members with an opportunity at least to read through it. In class a

student volunteers or is asked to read the selection to provide the class with a mutually experienced reading. Ideally the class has been striving to eliminate threat and fear within its communication system, so there should be little if any resistance to active student participation. Whatever fear may exist should dissipate once the work is led by the instructor and meaning-motivated students. But a *student* must always do the reading in a workshop exercising skills. Once an instructor reads to a class, even the most flexible student will to some extent accept the instructor's reading as a "model" at some level—conscious or unconscious—and some degree of emulation and imitation of the instructor's reading will follow; the students' creative efforts are at least partially aborted. The student communicators must do the experimental reading; the instructor must, with the class, help to guide the reader toward accurate control of meaning.

Once the selection is read, students immediately deal with any words needing clarification through precise definition and pronunciation; sometimes unfamiliar usage requires attention to prevent subsequent difficulties in rereading practice. In this selection any or all italicized words may require attention at least in the following areas: the name *Herzl* for pronunciation clarification; *chill* as a modifier rather than the more familiar verb (that is: Let's *chill* the apples); *vandals* and *ominously* for meaning and pronunciation; *pneumonia* for precise meaning and pronunciation; *orthopedic* for meaning and pronunciation; *welfare check* and *working class* for specific contextual meaning; *Puerto Rican* for pronunciation. In lines 9 and 10 the author places "on" after "stove" so that it is structurally possible for meaning to complete the action phrase "leaving . . . on"; or "on" may seem to introduce the phrase "24 hours a day." The reader must clarify the structural, compositional meaning to anticipate the possible confusion and avoid this possible trap in the oral presentation. The decoder must receive the message of "leave on" clearly from the reader's controlled oral delivery.

To solidify the denotative meaning of the words cited, and any other words that the students might question, descriptive language sources readily available should include the most recent unabridged and/or reliable abridged dictionary; Kenyon and Knott's useful guide, *The Pronunciation of American English;* and various other sources appropriate to the selection. Students should be encouraged to consult reference materials that take into consideration the students' verbal code in depth, works such as the comprehensive *Oxford English Dictionary*. Philology and etymology may provide a dimension of meaning unexpected in even the closest, analytical but unresearched items in the verbal code. Certainly, if Bob and his classmates (see transcript on pages 83–84) had been launched on an investigation of the history and usage of the word "prejudice," the pursuit might have led to fascinatingly pertinent activities. The more recent the writing, the more likely the accuracy of a student's personal definition, and aware oral readers should expect change in meaning through the pressure of major, world-wide events and widespread popular usage. Training in this area is vital for all aspects of accurate communication. In the excerpt from the *New York Times* few if any surprise meanings would be uncovered; researching of *vandals* might yield provocative material for future application, however. But students should be encouraged to investigate words used glibly and automatically, words such as "nice," "marvelous," "fabulous," and "terrific"; time has affected such usage considerably.

REREADING ALOUD

When denotative meaning has been thoroughly clarified, the selection should be reread in its entirety preferably by the same student. A basic principle of oral reading that must be recognized and applied in workshop preparation is the need for regular rereading, applying the knowledge and control gained since the previous rendering. In an effective communication system the verbal code is consistently questioned, clarified, and applied. This concept must pertain to oral reading as well. Students who at the outset of work in oral reading may cry, "Again?" grow to realize that meaning can only be clarified and controlled with *immediate* application to test for enlarged controlled meaning.

Upon completion of a second reading the workshop participants should state, as precisely as possible, the kernel meaning of the selection. The participating communicators should posit their ideas and limit their considered statements to the absolute minimum number of words; all members of the workshop should be satisfied with this "gloss," or "précis."[1] Having achieved agreement on core meaning, the class should check its results against a third reading of the selection aloud, the original reader being retained. Ideally, the same person should continue as the demonstration reader until a reading that qualifies as a satisfactory representation of the author's intention is achieved. What should be avoided is fragmentation of the selection by assigning new structural units—sentences, paragraphs—to different students. Working for logical, unified meaning through continuing oral control of the material must not be sacrificed to random multi-participation class techniques. The students

[1] Wayland Maxfield Parrish, *Reading Aloud* (New York: Ronald Press, 1966). Here and elsewhere in this chapter concepts and techniques are developed from experience with and application of Parrish's suggestions.

listening to the reader who is experimenting aloud must understand their particular, critical roles as decoders in the workshop process. Eventually everyone in the system may work as an encoder. But the teacher must work to discern evident growth in the control of applied skills by an individual working for improvement in the communications process.

By a third reading additional challenges become evident. Unity of logical meaning as worked out by the oral reader from the printed source must emerge for the listener. How has the writer organized the material to make his unified statement? In our first selection the author's design is clear and helpful: The first paragraph takes us from the street to the hallway, up the stairs of a partially occupied building to the apartment of a particular family of four; the second paragraph describes the cause and current status of the heating problem in the building; the third paragraph quotes the apartment's occupant on the ramifications of deprivation; the fourth paragraph amplifies our knowledge of health and well-being of the occupants, particularly the children; the fifth paragraph generalizes the particular situation, placing it in historical and sociological perspective.

THE ORAL READER'S VOICE

The reader with practice knows what is coming in the text and how it relates to what precedes. Therefore, through experimentation and guided practice, the reader's voice should be able to provide, for example, appropriate transition intonations that clarify the paragraphing for the listener. The voice of the reader, in dealing with the first paragraph, is guided by concentrated thinking that groups all the information in this paragraph as facts regarding the route to Mrs. Dickerson's apartment. When the route is completed, the reader's voice must indicate by appropriate adjustment of pitch, rate, intensity, and vocal quality that one aspect of the topic is concluded and another relative aspect is to begin. Transition is made. This conscious control becomes more noticeable and challenging at the beginning of the third paragraph; here the reader's voice must make it immediately clear to the listener that Mrs. Dickerson is speaking. How is this quotation indicated vocally? A usual, but often ineffective and distracting, technique is to intrude the words "quote" and "unquote." This is an evasion of vocal responsibility. The reader's *voice* must indicate the addition of the quotation. In this selection the use of the contraction "I'm" helps immediately. The reader must decide how the manipulation of elements of speech serves to clarify immediately upon utterance the meaning of each component of the carefully organized, written communication, including internal quotations.

In the fourth paragraph the writer links previous information to the living conditions of the Dickerson children. We have been told that the building is unheated; here we learn the baby had pneumonia. We have been told the "stairs groan ominously" as we climbed with the writer to the third floor of the building; now we are told one Dickerson child, who must use these stairs daily to get to school and return, "needs orthopedic care." Various items in the first and second paragraphs link with the statement: "All are in constant danger from the cold, from fires, from falling plaster. . . ." The skilled reader, through practice, controls the reading so that the fourth paragraph echoes and links meaning with specific information in the first, second, and third paragraphs.

As the reader ventures to produce a controlled unity, constructive criticism from the listeners as well as the reader's own self-evaluation should be hinged throughout on such questions as: Is reading rate appropriate to the subject matter throughout? Is pitch usage controlled for clarification and contrast of subject matter, for maintaining listener interest without distorting the writer's meaning? Does the reader's vocal quality project the attitude of the writer accurately? of Mrs. Dickerson in the quotation? Are vocal intensity, and loudness, controlled for acceptable listener audibility as well as being appropriate to the author's intention? Is this audibility level maintained throughout? Does the reader's breathing support audibility? Is the reader controlling diction so that words are always clear?

CONTROLLING THE ORAL READING

This conscious, close control of delivery may strike a beginning reader as mechanical, as intrusive rather than supportive to meaning. But the reader soon realizes—from the supportive verbal and nonverbal feedback from the listeners—that personal speech habits must be recognized and often altered when serving the meaning of another's written communication. Students with inefficient speech habits—who rush and slur words, who tend to whisper in conversation, who operate habitually at a pitch level that provides for little variation availablity, and so forth—soon learn the necessity of voice and diction control to serve meaning without apparent self-consciousness. Students may complain of feeling awkward as their inefficient habits are being adjusted to the needs of a reading, but they will realize through practice that new habits may be more efficient and, perhaps, more comfortable communication and that the listener suffers less and decodes more when the elements of speech are controlled. Reading aloud works as an excellent device for general speech improvement.

In order for the student reader to have full control of his manuscript while reading, he must learn to mark it to his needs with efficient, appropriate, easily decoded symbols. These markings must act as immediate reminders as the reading progresses; oral practice with such symbols marking the manuscript soon leads to comfortable, more closely controlled and accurate presentation. If the student knows phonetics, or knows a written system that can be used to help clarify individual phonemes (meaningful, minimal sound segments in a given language), diction can be clarified and produced at the articulation standard desired. Assume that a student reader has the following habits: beginning material at an inappropriate, arbitrary high-pitch level; dropping final consonant sounds; rushing inappropriately, particularly when basic, expository material is being presented. Such a student reader might mark the first paragraph of our illustrative manuscript for practice and ultimate presentation in the following manner:

Start at Optimum Pitch

```
                                          [l]      [z][z]  [k]  [d]
A   S      The narrow hallway in 102 Herzl Street is as dark and chill
P   [z]                           [d]     [t]                  [s]
P L  as the wintry street outside. Most of the apartments in the
R                                 [d] [d]     [t]              [z]
O O  building have been abandoned and stripped bare by vandals.
P             [z]                        [z]
R W  Plaster crumbles at the touch and the stairs groan ominously. On
I        [d]                                                   [z]
A    the third floor of this building Mrs. Nancy Dickerson lives with
T    her three children.
E
L
Y
```

When beginning work in oral reading, students may see little value in this technique; indeed, certain students may not need these manuscript reminders after enough practice secures the desired standard for presentation. But communicators eager for accuracy in message encoding and processing soon realize that previously unrecognized speech habits need conscious controlling; positive feedback from the teacher reinforces the reader's or speaker's attempts to manipulate speech elements consciously. Students who had been balking at this manuscript-marking technique were quick to recognize its effectiveness and importance when they visited the New York World's Fair in 1965 and viewed an exhibition of speech manuscripts delivered by President John F. Kennedy. The manuscripts were closely marked to help President Kennedy control those speech habits that might reduce the impact of the content in oral delivery. The student employing this technique not only controls the processing of the message more accurately but begins to listen—to himself and to others—more closely and discovers possible communication "noise" that was completely ignored heretofore. Distorted messages that have persisted in the communicator's most immediate, intimate environment may suddenly be recognized, analyzed and, at best, changed.

CONCENTRATION IN READING ALOUD

In reading aloud, the encoder should strive to maintain the *active* sense of communication that characterizes conversation under optimum conditions. Conversation at its best is not the idle, random chatter used to pass time; rather, conversation is the engaging of minds through words and gestures to promote creative, logical, well-supported, and ultimately exhilarating human interaction. The "conversational" attitude in reading demands that the verbal and nonverbal components be appropriate to the intentions of the person who originated the communication; implicit in the "conversational" method is active, responsible listening. Concentrated listening in a room can provide meaningful feedback as palpably as an active verbal response from the decoder. If a reader achieves an appropriate "conversational" level of delivery, the listener will never doubt that the speaker is engaged in spontaneous *thinking* while reading. The reader should avoid the mechanical, arbitrary delivery, which often provokes the negative feedback verbalized as, "You sound like you're reading," or a nonverbal response, the sight of listeners obviously bored, distracted, staring into space, and physically restless. To promote active response to the printed word, the reader generally should not memorize his material; for most oral interpreters the printed message remains spontaneous in delivery only as long as his concentration is focused on meaning; once this concentration shifts to remembering—which generally happens when a selection is memorized—concentration ceases. A listener is quick to recognize the absence or shift of concentration, whether he as decoder of the processed message has the time, skill, or opportunity to analyze and report his findings to the reader. When memorization is used, the transmission of the message becomes an *acting* rather than a *reading* problem.

Perhaps the most vivid indication of this occurs with many child actors, however talented. Once lines are memorized, the child's vocal delivery is automatic, devoid of thinking; the child's delivery is difficult to decode, since it is usually arbitrarily fast or deliberately slow and overarticulated; the message is simply a series of disconnected words.

This concentration, this "thinking-in," as certain teachers of oral interpretation phrase it, cannot be overstressed. Once the communication group or independent individual involved in an oral reading workshop situation has provided a précis for a given selection, this distilled statement of core meaning must be lodged in the thinking of the reader throughout the practice and delivery of the material. Each aspect of the reading—word, sentence, paragraph—must relate in the reader's mind to the unifying concept. The reader *must* think of what he is reading—word and idea—as he moves through the analyzed selection; if, while reading aloud, the encoder's mind jumps to the next sentence, the words and ideas being uttered at that moment will suffer in some definite way; perhaps arbitrary vocal delivery reducing meaning will testify to the sudden reduction of "thinking-in"; or word mispronunciation or word omission that leads to faulty language structure can produce the same results. The phrase "thinking-in" captures the required act, investing each aspect of the spoken communication with the quantity of concentrated thinking that produces an accurate communication. The serious communicator provides his "think-in" quality in his own spontaneous, conversational speaking. Here, too, however, the communication can be interrupted when thinking shifts momentarily; it is not uncommon, in a spontaneous dyad, for a momentarily distracted speaker to say, for example, "Three *months* ago, I arrived," when he meant to say, "Three *days* ago. . . ." The lack of continual concentration on the subject under discussion while speaking suddenly causes these substitutions, a kind of communication "noise." Usually, the encoder himself hears the error, or the decoder calls attention to the mistake; either way, the correction is made. If the speaker is distracted and cannot respond to the error in processing and if the decoder does not realize that an error has occurred, the inaccurate message may produce subsequent and sometimes serious ramifications. "Thinking-in" is obligatory for accuracy; in reading aloud, the reader's responsibility to the absent writer should underscore the requirement for deep concentration.

Furthermore, constructive criticism from the decoders involved should be hinged on their estimate of the degree to which the encoder is "thinking-in." Assume that the student reader had delivered the second sentence of the second paragraph, pausing briefly after the word "stove," providing the following phrasing: "The family has been without heat or hot water through most of the winter, and gets its only warmth by leaving the blackened gas stove [pause] on 24 hours a day." It is possible to "leave" the stove and go somewhere else for heat; but then the phrase "on 24 hours a day," though structurally possible in English, makes no sense here. If the reader has prepared the message and is "thinking-in" as he proceeds, he will anticipate the structural needs dictated by meaning in English to link "on" with "leaving" and make the necessary transition, with a pause if desired, but not required, after "on": ". . . and gets its only warmth by leaving the blackened stove on [vocal change] 24 hours a day." If the reader misreads in the workshop session, the listener can justly ask, "Were you 'thinking-in' while reading the second paragraph in your treatment of the use of 'on'?" If the proper working atmosphere exists within the workshop, no reader should become defensive at such a question; rather, the question should help the reader clarify the communication traps in the reading. Likewise, a decoder might question: "In your misreading of 'on,' had your thinking jumped to the beginning of the next paragraph, anticipating the challenge of delivering the transition into quoted material clearly?" Such specific questioning can be immediately helpful. Readers working for progress in a nonthreatening atmosphere will progress rapidly with this type of trained feedback; skills develop easily.

What must be avoided is an atmosphere in which a reader "performs" immediately, with the implicit hope that applause and generous statements of success and approval will follow. Students, when participating in "activities" such as oral reading in the classroom, are traditionally filled with general reactions like "That was very good" or "Marvelous!" The reading may have been "very good" or may even have had the quality of a "marvel," but such reactions help little if at all in gaining further skills. Certainly a student must never feel attacked by destructive comments, and the vocal delivery of the person asking critical questions in the workshop should implicitly project a desire and willingness to help the experimenting reader; vague generalities should be avoided. The ideal workshop is safe enough for the student so that he, himself, automatically rejects statements like "That was terrific—I really liked that reading." The student should be trained to retort, "Why? What, specifically, did you like"? The reader in search of constructive criticism must learn to challenge the attentive listener with such questions as, "What were the four (or however many) divisions into which the author divided his topic?" or "Were you able to hear all the words? I have a tendency to swallow ends of sentences" or "Did you consider my pausing arbitrary? Did the stopping intrude upon meaning?" Only with specific questions can the reader who is honing his skills measure the success of his communication—and the decoder's listening skills. This procedure builds the reader's security.

PUNCTUATION: ORAL AND WRITTEN

In trying to help students confront and solve possible problems in delivery, decoders' feedback—including the teacher's in a workshop—may be a recommendation that the reader "pay attention to punctuation." This message the experimenting reader may decode as "stop—take a pause—at each mark of punctuation"; indeed, this may be what the advice was intended to mean by those who gave it. But, in spontaneous speaking, do we "stop at punctuation"? If we were secretly to tape a lively discussion session and provide a transcript much like those used in this book, would every mark of punctuation—every period, comma, dash, exclamation point, and whatever—be represented on the spoken tape as a pause? Most assuredly not.

In oral language *all five* elements of speech work to clarify what written punctuation would clarify in writing; pause *may* be used meaningfully at the service of the *rate* element; but arbitrary pausing, without conscious, "think-in" purpose serves only to interrupt the thought unintentionally. To tell a student to stop when reading aloud at the comma, period, colon, and so on is to foster meaningless interruption, a form of destructive communication "noise." Indeed, traditionally some students are taught that the "period" means a "full stop." The teacher may have been referring to unity in written communication, but students automatically carry the concept into spoken language. The point is that no mark of punctuation dictates pause; rather, punctuation dictates relationship and attitude of ideas; ideally, punctuation on the printed page should relate what the selection would sound like were the author there to provide spoken input into the communication system. Woefully, what results too often from reading aloud, in class and out, is a recurrent vocal pattern with regular arbitrary pausing at punctuation, which we inaccurately label "singsong" or "monotone." It is neither singsong nor monotone but a student practicing what he has been mistaught about oral language.

If further proof for the purpose of punctuation is needed, listen to a professional recording of a famous, extemporaneously delivered speech or dialogue from a recorded play or recordings of literary value. As you listen, follow the selection in printed form. Punctuation does not dictate pause. Pause is used to underscore the meaning of previously uttered material or to anticipate and thereby enhance the meaning of ensuing language. These professionals on the recordings are interpreting the written word as if it were spoken. Language is *primarily* spoken and *secondarily* recorded in another form—telegraph, written language, pictures, smoke signals—when distance and time may impede the effectiveness of solely oral communication. In spontaneous, meaningful speech appropriately adjusted rate, intensity, quality, pitch (intonation pattern), and articulation and pronunciation can only be achieved when indicated by a written symbolic mark that we have come to call punctuation. Perhaps the word "punctuation" would be a good starting point for a communication system aimed at discovering what the words we use for communication really mean.

What do we really do when we punctuate? For the oral interpreter whose linguistic habits are so unconscious that they are difficult to discover, analyze, and evaluate, it may be helpful to prepare a manuscript devoid of formal English language punctuation, marked by the reader to indicate the manner in which the *voice* should guide the meaning. Ideally, this manuscript would be written phonetically so that the basic graphic representation would also be hinged on an awareness that *language is first and foremost spoken.* The student oral reader is generally filled with so many bad habits established and regularly reinforced that the factual mistakes need to be clarified and more accurate native language principles substituted. The oral reader, particularly if he distorts vowels due to regional, nonstandard, or foreign language elements in his American-English speech, must be trained to the awareness of vowels and consonants as primarily *spoken.* Check the descriptive language guide: the dictionary; for both words, "vowel" and "consonant," the *first* preferred definition given refers to the *sounds* and sound system of a given language.

Listen to the student reader reared on false rules and, although in spontaneous conversation that student practices accurate use of intonational pattern to project meaning, in oral reading the student sees a question mark on the page and whatever the structure of the sentence preceding the mark, the student's voice rises at the end of the utterance, and meaning is often arbitrarily, unconsciously distorted. Indeed, since the question mark spontaneously militates against useful "thinking-in," the student anticipates the end of the sentence, and the voice *begins* the sentence above an optimum or appropriate pitch level and arbitrarily continues to rise until the end of the sentence when the reader's pitch is not only too high for appropriate meaning but may be employing a pitch level that in English is rarely used except for emergency use, as in shouting, "Help! Fire!!"

A PROCEDURAL APPROACH

The oral reading student and the listeners guiding the constructive criticism in an oral interpretation workshop must have at least this minimal linguistic approach so that genuine "thinking-in" and skillful use of the reader's elements of speech will produce an accurate reading of the printed page congruent to the author's original intention. Consider the change in meaning of the following sentence (from the selection we have been using for workshop) when the word order is changed, a regular occurrence when "thinking-in" falters:

> Most of the apartments in the building have been abandoned and stripped bare by vandals.
> Most of the apartments in the building have been abandoned and bare stripped by vandals.
> Most of the apartments in the building have been abandoned and stripped by bare vandals.

In summary the classroom communication system involved in a workshop to develop skills in reading aloud should consider utilizing the following procedures to the appropriate degree:

1. Prepare the selection in manuscript form that is easily read and arranged for appropriate marking.
2. Begin with a student reading to provide the group with a mutual experience on which to base work toward organized control of the material.
3. One student should work with the material in workshop as long as progress is evident. *The teacher should never demonstrate useful or useless techniques.* The students must do the oral interpretation.
4. After the first reading clarify unknown or bewildering lexical items and usage. Clarify any other language problems.
5. Reread. Determine the core meaning of the selection by having the group work toward a distilled, minimal statement, a précis, of the author's intent.
6. Reread to check the accuracy of the group's précis. Remember that rereading with particular purpose and growing control is essential in the workshop. No selection can be reread too often if each reading provides a particular challenge. The decoder(s) should provide constructive criticism after each reading, based upon the purpose of the particular reading, hinged on knowledge of elements of speech.

7. Determine how the reader's elements of speech must serve intention. Consider the reader's personal voice and diction and how these may have to be closely controlled to serve the author. Mark the manuscript appropriately to help precise reading.

8. "Thinking-in," strong reading concentration, must be implicit in each reading. Listeners must provide constructive criticism to help the reader realize where, if anywhere, absence of "thinking-in" muffled the author's meaning. Let linguistic knowledge of American English support interpretation choices.

9. Practice enough to provide technical security so that the bulk of "thinking-in" is devoted to the author's ideas. Listeners provide constructive criticism.

10. When the reader has achieved a sensible rendering of the author's meaning, present the reading in its appropriate context. Let listener feedback, nonverbal primarily, help determine the efficiency, the achievement of the reading. The "success" of the reading might be measured by the degree to which the author's message is clear to the listener without the listener's conscious knowledge that the reader is manipulating, perhaps consciously, a variety of practiced skills. *What* the author says rather than *how* the reader says it is the really important quantity for the listener.

The initial literary selection considered for detailed workshop experimentation was a newspaper item that related an aspect of inner-city life. The selection may have helped a group of students involved in problem solving to illustrate an active malady—poverty—that must be faced in American life today. Now consider the following selection from *Truth of Intercourse* by Robert Louis Stevenson.[2] This excerpt is appropriate to the class working to analyze, evaluate, and understand the problems of verbal and nonverbal communication. The selection has been chosen to support man's historic concern with the components of communication; Stevenson capsulized this point in history when the machine was making dehumanizing inroads in man's daily life. (Italics are ours for subsequent reference.)

Truth of Intercourse

Life is not entirely carried on by *literature*. We are
subject to physical *passions* and *contortions;* the voice
breaks and changes, and speaks by unconscious and winning

[2] *Ibid.,* pp. 80–81.

inflections; we have legible *countenances,* like an open
book; things that cannot be said look *eloquently* through 5
the eyes; and the soul, not locked into the body as a *dungeon,*
dwells ever on the *threshold* with appealing *signals.* Groans
and tears, looks and *gestures,* a *flush* or a paleness, are often
the most clear reporters of the heart, and speak more directly
to the hearts of others. The message flies by these interpreters 10
in the least space of time, and the misunderstanding is *averted*
in the moment of its birth. To explain in words takes time and
a just and patient hearing; and in the *critical epochs* of a close
relation, patience and justice are not qualities on which
we can rely. But the look of gesture explains things in a 15
breath; they tell their message without *ambiguity.* . . .
    Pitiful is the case of the blind, who cannot read the face;
pitiful that of the *deaf,* who cannot follow the changes of the
voice. And there are others also to be pitied; for there are some
of an *inert, uneloquent* nature, who have been denied all the *sym-* 20
bols of communication, who have neither a lively play of facial
expression, nor speaking gestures, nor a responsive voice, nor
yet the gift of *frank,* explanatory speech: people truly *made of clay,*
people *tied for life into a bag* which no one can undo. Such people
we must learn slowly by the *tenor* of their acts, or through 25
yea and nay communications; or we take them on trust on the strength
of *a general air,* and now and again, when we see the *spirit*
breaking through in a flash, correct or change our *estimate.*
But these will be uphill *intimacies,* without charm or freedom, to
the end; and freedom is the chief ingredient in confidence. 30
Some minds, *romantically dull,* despise physical *endowments.*
That is a *doctrine* for a *misanthrope;* to those who like their
fellow *creatures* it must always be meaningless; and, for my part,
I can see few things more desirable, after the possession
of such *radical* qualities as honor and humor and pathos, than 35
to have a lively and not a *stolid* countenance; to have looks to
correspond with every feeling; to be *elegant* and delightful in
person, so that we shall please in the intervals of active
pleasing, and may never *discredit* speech with *uncouth* manners
or become unconsciously our own *burlesques.* But of all 40
unfortunates there is one creature (for I will not call him man)
conspicuous in misfortune. This is he who has *forfeited* his
birthright of expression, who has cultivated *artful intonations,*
who has taught his face tricks, like a pet monkey, and on every

side *perverted* or cut off his means of communication with   45
his fellow-men. The body is a house of many windows: there
we all sit, showing ourselves and crying on the passers-by
to come and love us. But this fellow has filled his window
with *opaque* glass, elegantly colored. His house may be admired
for its design, the crowd may pause before the *stained windows*,   50
but meanwhile the poor proprietor must lie *languishing* within,
uncomforted, unchangeably alone.

This lengthy selection would extend over several pages if reproduced
to facilitate reading aloud but a typed, wide-margined arrangement is
still advisable. The italicized language elements all need clarification; but
students, particularly if they have a basis in communication training,
might research the language and usage independently so that decision
making concerning appropriate contextual meaning could occupy their in-
class time. Although some fifty-one words or phrases are noted above for
possible consideration, the communication system that has chosen the
Stevenson material might find additional items worth investigating and
certain of those recommended here less important. However, because this
material was written in the late nineteenth century but vitally retains
attitudes regarding human relationships that are central to our thinking
today, the manner of communicating such attitudes deserves close attention. The abundance of language items that need clarification might
provide the in-class communication systems with problem solving, small
group activities hinged on the challenge of reading such material aloud.
The small groups could explore such questions as: What is "literature"? Is
the language of *Truth of Intercourse* our current American-English
language? What varying attitudes does Stevenson project, and can our
twentieth-century mind and voice capture these attitudes accurately for a
listener? But whatever the approach and however the guide of ten listed
suggestions may be employed in a particular communication system,
Stevenson provides this challenge to concerned communicators: With
precision and controlled intelligence communicate by carefully structured
and consciously designed ideas on human contact through verbal and
nonverbal communication.

With Stevenson's *meaning* always central to the oral communicator's
"thinking-in" approach, the immediate challenge of the verbal code is
evident; such items as "intercourse," "literature," "inflections," "gestures,"
and "epochs," to cite several in the initial paragraph, contrast and change
in common usage through the intervening years, which is a real problem;
but accurate pronunciation to assure clarity of meaning should also be a
real consideration. Confusion of "epochs" with "epics," for example, could
provide difficulties that contextual meaning might not clarify spontane-

ously during the oral presentation of the selection. Since Stevenson provides a continual challenge to meaning at this level in *Truth of Intercourse,* the material becomes a valuable exercise in precise transmission of another's meaning; the verbal code must be controlled at a clearly defined denotative level by the encoder. The twentieth-century encoder might encounter ambiguity often; distortion of meaning is possible, unless the reader, the decoder, controls the denotative meaning through disciplined processing. The encoder's "thinking-in" and manipulation of elements of speech must be consistently at the service of Stevenson. This control may become even more crucial when suddenly Stevenson uses a formal metaphor of standard, nineteeth-century English in line 24, "tied for life into a bag," which may remind a youthful twentieth-century encoder of a popular colloquial expression (in use at the time of this book's writing and perhaps already disappearing from spoken English): "I know his behavior seems strange and different; but that's his bag, and he's got to do his thing." If the encoder confuses the two "bags," and if some detectable feedback does not inform the encoder of this "noise," parts of the ensuing message may be distorted, however controlled and expert the oral processing.

Not the least of the challenges is the encoding and processing of the verbal code in lines 32 through 40, this one long grammatical structure we call a single sentence. Assume that the reader has managed an accurate delivery of Stevenson's meaning to this point with the help of disciplined concentration and appropriately applied voice and diction. Assume also that the italicized items (*doctrine, misanthrope, creatures, stolid, elegant, discredit, uncouth, burlesques*) have all achieved accurate meaning in Stevenson's context through experimentation and honing of the oral communicator's skills in a communication system that he, as encoder, understands in depth. One italicized item in the verbal code remains: *radical.* How does the encoder read this word to project its precise meaning *in this context?* What meaning did you assign to *radical* when reading the selection? Try an additional experiment, one already suggested in the treatment of Bob's use of "prejudice": After reading through the material aloud at least once with all the communicators listening (whether "communicators" here means only the reader working alone employing his personal subsystems as he reads or a larger system in a class workshop), jot down the meaning of *radical;* try to provide one word, a synonym.

When this experiment was tried in a university class in oral interpretation in 1970, a communication system in which diversity of student "majors" ranged from physical education to physics and mathematics, the shared results were not surprising: *radical* meant "extreme," "way out," "communistic," "holding minority political viewpoints," and the like. All definitions reflected the students' immediate, involved, twentieth-century experience. Substitute "extreme" for *radical* in Stevenson's context: ". . . I can see few things more desirable, after the possession of such *extreme* qualities as honor and humor and pathos, than to have a lively and not a stolid countenance; . . ." If we accept this current definition, what happens to Stevenson's attitude? Is he meaning to be humorous, perhaps even sarcastic to make his point? Certainly, *radical* meaning "extreme" would assure an attitude less direct, more available for communication distortion, than the material preceding this utterance would suggest. If undistorted basic meaning without the complication of varying attitudes is Stevenson's aim, and accuracy of encoding and processing is the reader's goal, what else could *radical* mean here? The dictionary indicates that *radical* in its most primary, limited denotation means "root," "fundamental," or "basic." And isn't this Stevenson's usage here, that the desirable things for man are the basic, the fundamental, the root "qualities": "honor and humor and pathos . . ."? Often, the words most critical—and therefore most dangerous—to accurate understanding of meaning in reading aloud—and every form of verbal communication— are words that we take for granted; we automatically accept our own modern, connotation-loaded meanings for those of a writer or a speaker.

If the encoder receives *radical* as "extreme," what happens to the rest of Sevenson's communication? Either it is scuttled by subsequent inaccurate attitude projection (sarcastic, ironic), or it provokes useless confusion that jeopardizes all aspects of subsequent accurate decoding. The reader must discover through workshop experimentation how "thinking-in" and masterful, precise oral delivery capture Stevenson's intention. Remember: The silent reader as decoder of *Truth of Intercourse* can go back, stop, look up the word, clarify confusion with the help of additional time. The silent reader controls his own encoding and processing. The listener has *one chance,* and this chance is at the mercy of time—and the oral reader as encoder! In workshop the oral reader might experiment with nonverbal as well as verbal aids to meaning. Does a spontaneous gesture seem to help the meaning of *radical?* Would direct eye contact with the decoder during the processing of the crucial part of the message help, perhaps, during the section ". . . I can see few things more desirable, after the possession of such radical qualities as honor and humor and pathos . . ."? Or, in the final judgment, will the ultimate burden for accurate meaning depend on: the "thinking-in" of *radical* as "fundamental"; the conveyance of serious attitude; and appropriate intensity, rate, pitch, quality, articulation, pronunciation?

The verbal code in this section of *Truth of Intercourse* demands clarity because beyond the individual word the oral reader must convey grace-fully this complicated, lengthy sentence in a carefully structured paragraph. The reader's voice must meet the oral challenge of one sentence that, to the decoder, might logically divide into two sentences. That is, Stevenson's punctuation must guide oral delivery; the writer's use of the semicolon and comma must be rendered accurately. Note that the grammatical structure through "misanthrope" comprises the conventional English sentence; but a semicolon, not a period, is used; likewise through "countenance" and the second semicolon. Thereafter, the conventional English sentence structure is abandoned, and sentence fragments occur between semicolons until the sentence's conclusion with "burlesques" and the period. To complicate this structure further for the oral reader, Stevenson punctuates subordinated and/or amplified ideas with generous use of the comma. Perhaps the greatest vocal challenge in delivery of the sentence is the reader's appropriate use of intonation pattern (pitch) and rate where Stevenson uses the semicolon. The sentence from beginning to end must have the complex unity Stevenson provides. The unskilled reader (if this teacher's experience serves accurately), unconsciously, automatically provides the sentence-ending intonation pattern and an arbitrary pause when reading the semicolon. In Stevenson's sentence such treatment would fragment the idea but retain some substantial meaning through "countenance" and the third semicolon. But then the remainder of the utterance—two incompleted utterances separated by a semicolon—might cause confusion in the decoding. The listener could not be expected to solve the structural problem on the spot. The decoding for the remainder of the selection would at best be confused, at worst end in chaos and communication frustration. The reader's skills must serve: his concentration of thought; his understanding and grasp of what material follows as well as what has preceded and what is encoded and processed at the moment; and his artful application of appropriate voice and diction achieved through workshop experimentation.

It is hard work for the encoder to gain the unity Stevenson has provided in this selection; it is hard work for the encoders who must understand the listener's responsibilities. Skilled processing of the oral communication, however, pays off for all members of the system with Stevenson's concluding remarks (lines 40 through 52): An encoder's self-conscious verbal and nonverbal "tricks . . . cut off his means of communication with his fellow-men." A life of loneliness results. Only through honest, accurate, open communication can man touch man. This concept was crucial for Stevenson as he experienced the Industrial Revolution a century ago. It is crucial for us as we confront the "revolutions" of the Space Age.

To summarize what has been said thus far in the practice and theory of communication systems as applied to the classroom, analyze and evaluate the following two transcript segments recorded on video tape from the same junior high school communication system. Unfortunately the printed page does not provide the sound, or the picture, part of the original processing. But the transcripts should provide sufficient input for fundamental considerations regarding the use of reading aloud in the classroom oriented to modern communication systems.

TRANSCRIPT SEGMENT ONE

Teacher: All right. I want to read you some more things, and then I want to try something. And absorb this stuff. I want it to come in. I want you to feel it because when we're done, we'll try something. This is called "Dream Deferred."[3]

> *What happens to a dream deferred*
>
> Does it dry up
> like a raisin in the sun?
>
> Or fester like a sore—
> And then run?
> Does it stink like rotten meat?
> Or crust and sugar over—
> like a syrupy sweet?
>
> Maybe it just sags
> like a heavy load.
>
> Or does it explode?

Teacher: Yes? What?

Child: When something explodes that's big, like a ball. . . . (*Voice becomes indistinguishable.*)

Teacher: Is that what happens to a dream?

Child: No.

Teacher: Why do you think he uses those words? Why do you think he compares it to a cut?

Child: I don't really know, but when I dream, it don't stink.

Teacher: You want to hear that one again? All right. I'm gonna read these things straight. Oh, it's called *Children's Rhymes*. All right. Let's listen to this. Let's hear this *Children's Rhymes*.[4]

---

[3] "Dreams Deferred" by Langston Hughes. Reprinted by permission of A. A. Knopf. Also by permission of Harold Ober Associates, Inc.

[4] From *The Panther and the Lash* by Langston Hughes. Reprinted by permission of A. A. Knopf. Also by permission of Harold Ober Associates, Inc.

> By what sends the white kids, I ain't sent
> I know I can't be president.
> What don't bug them white kids sure bugs me
> We know everybody ain't free.
> What's written down for white folks ain't for us a—all
> "Liberty and justice—huh—For all." For all?

What do you think of that?

Child: I think it's good because most people just make up poems. . . . (*Voice becomes indistinct.*)

Teacher: Do you think the poem's true? Do you think when he says, "By what sends the white kids, I ain't sent. I know I can't be president"—do you think that's true?

Child: Yes.

Teacher: Do you believe that? Let me ask you a question. Do you think this poem is true? (*Relating to the students*) You think it's true. You don't think it's true. Why don't you think it's true?

Child: Some of it is true, but like some things that he say, to me aren't true. Because like what he says what white kids not thinking about. He's thinking about let's have truth, but he said you couldn't be president. You could be president if people just believed in you.

Teacher: Thank you. Does anybody else think the poem is—what do you think about the poem?

Child: Well, I think we should get a chance to be president, too, some of us, too, instead of the white people, too.

Teacher: Do you think that's gonna happen some day?

Child: Yes. And I think the poem is true.

Teacher: You think the poem is true?

Child: Yes.

Child: I think that if we stay together, some time one day we'll all be free together.

Child: I think the poem is true because the way you read it, it seems like it's true a lot.

Teacher: Do you think you could be president some day?

Child: Nope! I don't want to be.

Teacher: What do you want to be?

Child: I want to be a plain old man, working.

TRANSCRIPT SEGMENT TWO

Teacher: All right. I found another turtle poem. I want to see if you like it better. This is by a young black woman who's a poet, and I want to see if you like this turtle poem any better. All right? Than the other turtle. I have to find it. Here. It's called "The

Emancipation of George Hector." Who knows what "emancipation" means? Do you know? What? (*Inaudible response*) No,
"emancipation." Have you heard of the Emancipation Proclamation? Abraham Lincoln? What's "emancipation" mean? (*Inaudible student response*) That's right. He says it's a . . . it
has to do with freedom. The word itself means to free somebody, and the proclamation was the paper Abraham Lincoln
signed which declared the slaves free. So, this is called "The
Emancipation of George-Hector," a colored turtle. There's only
one word in here I think would probably be difficult, which is a
word, "languorous," which means lazy. That's all.

The Emancipation of George-Hector[5]

George Hector is spoiled.
Formerly he stayed well up in his shell
But now he hangs arms and legs sprawlingly in a most
  languorous fashion.
Headward back to be admired, he didn't use to talk,
But he does now.

Do you like that turtle poem better than your turtle poem? Why
do you like it better? Why do you like that turtle poem better?

Child: I think it's a very good poem because it tells you more things
           about the turtle than the other story.
Teacher: What kinds of things does it tell you about the turtle that the
           other poem didn't tell?
Child: It tells about, it just tells about the turtle and what he does dur-
           ing the day. The other one had lots of jokes, but this one tells
           more about the turtle than any other story I've heard about
           George.
Teacher: Does anybody have any . . . what kind of things does it say
           about the turtle?
Child: It says he is colored. (*Voice indistinct*)
Teacher: Go ahead.
Child: In that story they say more interesting things than in the turtle
           story 'cause they have easy words in the turtle story, but in
           this. . . . (*Voice fades.*)
Teacher: One more.
Child: How the turtles talk about. . . . (*Voice fades.*)
Teacher: All right. I want to read you some more things. Then I want to
           try something. And absorb this stuff. I want it to come in. I
           want you to feel it because when we're done, we're gonna try
           something.

[5] The Emancipation of George-Hector by Mari E. Evans. From *American Negro
Poetry*, Arna Bontemps (New York: Hill and Wang, 1964). Reprinted by permission.

Eight

Integrating Language Experiences: Communication Games

Communication games consist of simulated life experiences in the classroom workshop. Their aim is to help the communicator investigate his storehouse of sense memory and to provide new experiences so that his ever-growing perceptual field will relate readily to whatever experience life provides beyond the workshop. "Games" comprise serious concentrated behavior with defined and accepted rules that the players must respect. Progress in a game reflects an understanding of these rules by the players and mutual respect of the players for each other. All life experience proceeds according to rules, some clearly defined and written down, some loosely defined and tacit, and many lying somewhere in between. To recognize these rules and to work within them, practicing focused concentration, is to proceed with continual discovery to a point where you can make a reasonable evaluation about how you played the game and the degree of success you achieved. If the rules of the game are untenable and unreasonable after the players have attempted the game and evaluated the problems, then the rules might be changed or altered; but the accepted rules, once agreed upon, generally allow the players genuine freedom in a sensible structure providing growth, discovery, and the natural product of these two, enjoyment.

125

A word of caution is necessary here: Communication games employ the investigation and use of human senses, and self-awareness is central in a growing understanding of others. But the games are not meant to be used as a springboard for group psychotherapy. Communication games are used to create a mutual experience for a systemic analysis of the communication shared within the system. They center on the "here and now" rather than on factors from the past that influence the "here and now."

ADVANTAGES OF COMMUNICATION GAMES

Communication games have several advantages in the communication-oriented classroom. The first is that they provide a structure that is usable for system analysis. The rules that are necessary to the playing of the game become, during the postgame evaluation period, the framework on which analysis takes place. The rules constitute built-in criteria of success; if a rule is not followed, a breakdown takes place that affects the communication processing. By starting analysis with an investigation of the players' adherence to rules, the analyst avoids the tendency merely to talk about an event in general terms of good and bad and begins evaluating the process factors and their effects on the event.

Second, the game, by its limitation in time and number of players, is a complete communication event—a closed system. The game is a unified experience rather than a series of disjointed and possibly unrelated "learning" experiences. Because it is a closed system, students are able to observe the effects of many variables on an outcome that is complete and fully known. In life situations we are ordinarily forced to analyze ongoing events with indistinguishable outcomes.

Third, the communication games simulate life through the use of rules. In his book *Encounters* Erving Hoffman writes about the rules that control interpersonal relationships and labels them "rituals." He says:

> The process of mutually sustaining a definition of the situation in face-to-face interaction is socially organized through rules of relevance and irrelevance. These rules for the management of engrossment appear to be an insubstantial element of social life, a matter of courtesy, manners and etiquette. But it is to these flimsy rules, and not to the unshaking character of the external world, that we owe our unshaking sense of realities. To be at ease in a situation is to be properly subject to these rules. . . .[1]

[1] Erving Hoffman, *Encounters* (Indianapolis, Ind.: Bobbs-Merrill, 1961), pp. 80–81.

Since rules or rituals exist in all our interpersonal relationships, the game is a practice period for real life communication. More important, because it is a game set up in the neutral area, the playing field of the classroom, students can analyze their interaction in detail without fear that their possible discoveries about themselves or their fellow communicators will influence permanent relationships.

Time and patience are necessary on the part of the teacher-facilitator because the student communicators will not immediately function freely as game players. Communicators must be trained to have confidence in their responses within the situations. Games based on self-awareness through concentration speed up the realization of this confidence, and because everyone is experiencing intensity of involvement, group cohesion begins to evolve. Only then will games really begin to show results.

In addition, communication games provide confirmed data supporting the basic tenets of interpersonal communication. Students who are involved in the games—as players or spectators—cannot help but learn that all behavior involves sending messages to someone else and that responses are continually being decoded. It also becomes obvious to the communicators that every message carries content information and information about the relationship between the people who are interacting. Every message not only tells how you are feeling at the moment but how you feel toward and about the person to whom you are communicating. As we showed at length earlier in this book, most of the relationship information or data are carried in paralinguistic and nonverbal aspects of messages. It is this relationship aspect of the message that determines whether the people who are communicating are either in parallel positions or whether one person is "one up" on the other—that is, whether the relationships are symmetrical or complementary. All these principles can be isolated, identified, and discussed within the game context.

In summary, human behavior is being exercised within the human relations laboratory known as the classroom. Verbal and nonverbal activities—games—provide a mutual life space for communicators to discover how the process of learning occurs; how, from a clearly established, relatively simple set of rules, the individual or group can progress within defined limits, trusting the system and its rules as progress is made, and concluding with a "discovery."

This discovery may be valuable in and of itself; more often, the discovery provides a mutuality of experience, which enables the participant(s) to proceed to a more complex and revealing "game." In such games the "players"—the human beings experiencing life's roles—must respect the limitations and the participant; must keep faith with the communication system at work—at "play"—so that these involved communicators can make discoveries as the game progresses. The outcome of an honestly played game is never anticipated; it develops; it is discovered from the process as the players contribute. If the player agrees on his immediate limitations for a particular game, the rules can be freeing, for they provide a sense of security. The player will learn to respond totally—through all senses—and spontaneously. The rules of the game will help the participant discover who he is, where he is, when the experience occurred, what happened. The "how"—the method used—will evolve as the ultimate discovery; but the "how" only comes through the playing and not in anticipating the outcome. The "why"—the justification for the activity—is eventually implicit in each game played.

In communication games limits should not be confused with barriers. Limits constitute boundaries that the players respect so that once achieving the final boundary and solving the problem of the particular game, the participant is ready to move on to the next game, to a farther boundary that exists to be met and, eventually, gone beyond. A barrier, however, suggests a wall, a restricting device that prevents or discourages future mobility or extension; there is a sense of permanent physical conclusion about a barrier that is not true of a boundary, or limit. If a student recognizes the distinction, he understands the concept of limits.

Communication games should not be thought of as being restricted to the very young or to those taking advanced theater courses. Rather, the games approach demonstrates learning in action, whatever the academic discipline and grade level; games are adaptive. Even if the games orientation seems inimical, say, to the possible methods of teaching the sciences, simply consider the fact that the traditional science classroom is forced to be an experimental laboratory. Students explore possibilities and draw limited conclusions based on personal involvement and observation of the process about which a hypothesis was framed. The spirit of the game is implicit in good science teaching; that often the result of much science teaching is unassimilated rote and isolated factual data attests to problems in teaching methods and misinterpretation of student needs. But whatever the teacher-facilitator's response to the literal use of games within the classroom, the purpose of the games cannot be denied if the learning process is understood: to allow the communicator to discover—at an appropriate rate, without the anxiety generated by fearful, highly competitive, judgmental environment—how to solve definite problems with recognized limits.

The representative games included here are the results of years of experimentation by dedicated facilitators, experimentation that continues today. Leaders in this human workshop approach have been loath to provide written description of the games for fear that readers—particularly tradition-bound teachers—will use the "activities" most easily understood and executed during an available few minutes that need "filling" in the linear-structured, conventional class day. All communicators in a particular communication system must realize the organic nature of the games structure, the manner in which the games feed each other. In this sense the teacher is genuinely a facilitator, and student-teacher relationships become clearly defined as symmetrical. The teacher must be willing to take the time that the students need to find the game's intention.

The books that have recorded the work of the leaders in this area demonstrate the problem: Grace Stanistreet's *teaching is a dialogue*[2] is a sixty-eight page book that took over thirty years to write, despite continual urging and professional pressure, because the teacher as facilitator is so central to the approach that Miss Stanistreet may feel that the written word, illuminating though it is, is clearly insufficient. Viola Spolin's *Improvisation for the Theater*[3] numbers some 400 pages that she terms a "handbook" to help facilitators tune in to the method. Spolin's diligent detail suggests that it is easy to go wrong if games are not clearly understood and intelligently facilitated. Ideally, theater games users should emerge from workshops designed and taught by these two women or their trained disciples. Indeed, if either is available, arrange a workshop and learn firsthand. When city-wide tests revealed that the student reading levels had declined dangerously after an extended teachers' strike in a major American city, an acting superintendent of schools probed the problem further and suggested, "It isn't the technique that you use, it's the way the teacher knows the technique. . . ." Certainly this is true in all classrooms; it is especially true in the communications system using games in the classroom laboratory to simulate life experiences.

The following games may make sense to communicators in a definite order; but the needs of an individual class should determine the use of a particular game in a particular communication system. Also, the facilitator should understand the value of repeating a game at useful intervals to apply insights achieved subsequent to the initial playing and to develop new limits and additional human relationships.

---

[2] Grace M. Stanistreet, *teaching is a dialogue* (Adelphi University, Garden City, N.Y., 1969). This chapter owes much, in approach, to this volume and application of materials gained from work with Margaret A. Linney, a former student and colleague of Grace M. Stanistreet.

[3] Viola Spolin, *Improvisation for the Theater* (Evanston, Ill.: Northwestern University Press, 1963). The philosophy and approach of this chapter are greatly indebted to this volume.

The games here are descriptive of an approach, not prescriptive and therefore necessarily incomplete. Those included are meant to be *illustrative*. They are based on the Stanistreet-Spolin materials. The physical space for experience with communication games, for optimum participation, should be a large open area that can easily accommodate the participants if all are simultaneously engaged in a game that requires generous, free-wheeling movement; this is a kind of playing field. The students' movable chairs should be arranged in semicircular fashion to form the outer limit at one end or one part of the open space. The chairs should be accessible for games as needed; the seated communicators should always have ready visual access to all members of the system. It cannot be stressed too strongly that the teacher-facilitator who chooses to try communication games to simulate life experience in the classroom must have established a working rapport in the communication system that would allow virtually any experiment in human action and interaction to occur freely without threat of censure or judgment. The student participants must willingly try techniques to expand and explore self-awareness, to build the class's mutual life space. Students and teacher alike must constantly work to avoid traditional, prejudiced, often automatic responses to their lives in and out of the classroom. A childhood game may be as useful to simulate particular meaningful group or individual behavior as a simulation that works toward the investigation and understanding of a community's racial prejudice. All participants must suspend judgment, analyze, and proceed with a mutually experienced and ever-growing fund of human data.

GAME ONE

Desired Outcome: To discover and establish group and individual identity; to begin to build group and individual faith; to begin establishing a mutual life space imaginatively.

Rules of the Game:
1. From the outset concentrate on classmates' participation.
2. Remember the aim is not memorization but a building of faith in your fellow classmates and a willingness to participate when you are ready. Work to clarify "who" these people are.
3. Willingly provide help if classmates falter when your name comes up.

4. Risk being imaginative with people you hardly know. Remember—group cohesion is important.
5. Don't write. Just listen and watch.
6. Make no judgments about the game's isolated usefulness. Be willing to proceed.

Sample Game: "My Grandmother went to California, and in her trunk she packed . . ."

The participants are seated in the semicircle. The facilitator begins by saying the above sentence aloud, concluding it with his or her first name and an item that begins with the same initial sound as the person's name (Jessica and ginger; Rick and rhubarb). A student then volunteers to join the game by repeating the previous person's completed sentence and adding his own name and item (Mary and mustard). The game proceeds until each class member has added to the contents of grandmother's trunk, reiterating the names and items, if possible, in the order of deposit. No written notes may be taken during this game (or indeed during any communication game). The participant must concentrate on each contributor and his contribution and maintain faith in his own ability to remember. If a volunteer forgets names and/or items after an honest attempt to remember, he may ask for help from the group member whose name and/or item he forgot. Students should not offer aid by calling out the forgotten items. In the hypothetical class of thirty students and one facilitator the final participant in the game would repeat the sentence and include thirty names with appropriate items before adding his own.

Systems Evaluation: This game, played in a seated position for initial comfort and physical security, immediately requires the student to recognize the importance of controlled concentration in game playing. Concentration that leads to success is often discussed in education but too rarely understood. As this game progresses, the group's intensification of individual and pooled concentration becomes almost palpable. The team spirit develops. The game serves as an introductory device after which students rarely forget each other—and often they greet each other laughingly, using the item rather than the name: "Hello, rhubarb!" Quickly a communal commitment is achieved by many system participants and a basic level of trust through sharing as well. Students who are fearful may wait to volunteer; this may build fear temporarily, but eventual participation generally pays off with even the most anxious student responsive to how faith in himself and willingness to receive group help in time of need provides a self-generating security. Possible game variations might be: "pack" a nonsense word (gloop, flootch, glurg); an abstraction or human value (a joyous smile, a soothing spring blueness, civil rights). Let the game begin to liberate the imagination and language; choice of item will begin to reflect the thinking of the participants. It will begin to provide insights, verbal and nonverbal for the communicators in this mutual life space. In the best sense communicators begin to expose themselves and their backgrounds.

GAME TWO

Desired Outcome: To discover a personal storehouse of memory for immediate and subsequent application to interpersonal problem solving.

Rules of the Game:

1. Restrict concentration to your own body. Block out all reception of sensory messages except the sound of the facilitator's voice. Establish yourself as the "who."
2. Don't talk. Let only the facilitator's "side coaching" be heard.
3. Work until you literally feel the desired sensation to the degree that you are able.
4. Do not judge success or failure of your untrained abilities on the evidence of this first attempt.
5. Be willing to try again.
6. Make no judgments about the game's isolated usefulness. Be willing to proceed.
7. Be honest in group evaluation of individual feelings.

Sample Game: Sensory Awareness Games

Each student sits in his chair, feet firmly on the ground, eyes closed; there is no speaking except by the facilitator. The student concentrates as fully as possible on the floor to get a definite awareness of the pressure of the floor on the soles of his shoes; he then shifts concentration to the pressure of the sole on the stocking or sock; once the literal feeling of the pressure is achieved through focused concentration, he moves to the stocking-foot pressure; then trousers or skirt pressure at the point where contact is made on the body; then undergarments against the body; outergarments over undergarments against the body. As facilitator you have the communicators continue the route, coaching them until all possible pressures that exist are explored through continued, uninterrupted concentration. When the feelings of pressures on the body are explored and the participants have been introduced to their own feeling, instruct them to rise and move across the playing field and concentrate on the pressure, the feeling of the air around the moving body; vary the rate of motion to provide varying air pressures. Suggest that the participants imagine that there is a wind storm and they are walking against the wind; let the body respond to the imagined pressure; add snow to the wind; let the body, through memory of these experiences, respond accordingly. Hold concentration. Possible sensory recall variations (with eyes closed to help concentration) might be: Hold a piece of imaginary wet soap in hand. How big is it? What is its shape? texture? weight? color? smell? Explore it. Add other senses. Now go back to the last outdoor sports event you attended. See the entire place. How large is the arena? How many people? What are the colors? How vivid is the sky? Is it bright blue? cloudy? What are the colors of the uniforms of the teams? Clarify each color aspect of the memory image. Add sound. Are the spectators shouting? Is there a hush of expectancy? Are the sounds shrill? Add temperature. Is it cold? Are you bundled in clothing? Do you feel cold against your face? wind? Is it hot? Is the sun oppressive? comfortably warming? Are you perspiring? Is there a cool breeze? Feel the breeze. Is there a food smell in the air? Does the air smell of the season? Take a bite of a crisp apple. Is it sweet? Is it juicy? Is it too big a bite? What is the texture of the apple? Can you smell the apple? chew it? Is it getting softer? Can you hear the chewing? Do you feel the apple against your teeth as you chew? against your tongue? Chew the bite of apple until it is ready to be swallowed. Swallow it. Can you feel it in your esophagus as it descends? Is it in your stomach? Can you feel it there?

Systems Evaluation: These games continue training concentration, here to sharpen sensory response through memory of familiar, perhaps recurrent, but often ignored experience. Concentration must be sharply focused if sensations are to be realized. Rushing through such a game diminishes its seriousness. The student must build faith in himself in his attempt to recapture a particular taste, smell, feeling, sound. This takes time and patience. The facilitator should coach aloud, guiding with meaningful questions. If the student is holding concentration, he can train himself to focus on the experience and still follow directions and guidance. This "side coaching," as Spolin calls it, may depend on the facilitator's responses to nonverbal cues that the students are providing through spontaneous physicalization. Side coaching is useful throughout communication games once the student begins to understand the nature of concentrated attention. Although the individual student holds independent concentration, the presence of the group, with each member working for sensory recall through concentration, provides a tacit security that soon dissipates the self-consciousness the individual participator might experience. Furthermore, group discussion and detailed evaluation of their sensory recall and depth of concentration conducted after the game or at the end of a game session should provide students with vivid insights into the vast variety of recalled experiences possible from, "Take a bite of an apple. Chew it." Students will share contrasting experiences and soon, if not immediately, share additional past experiences triggered by the reexperiencing of a sense memory. Backgrounds and perceptual fields will be exposed and shared, little by little. The nonverbal game allows for subsequent sharing through verbalization. Students begin to take risks with each other.

GAME THREE

**Desired
Outcome:**   To discover the detail of commonplace human behavior and the importance of precise sensory involvement in human behavior.

**Rules of
the Game:**   1. Establish concentration. Be in a particular space doing a definite act. The "who" is the individual, and the "what" doing the act.
2. Do not speak. Listen to side coaching but focus on involvement in own behavior.
3. As "direction" changes, try to make a quick and appropriate sensory adjustment.
4. Allow yourself enough time to literally see, smell, taste, feel, hear.
5. Don't become discouraged if one sense seems stronger than others.
6. Be willing to proceed and to build concentration.
7. If you speak, allow the words to come from the activity. Don't tell anyone—including yourself—what you are doing. Show.

Sample Game: Directions

Everyone stands, randomly arranged, in the playing area. Each participant allows enough space to avoid a sense of crowding. When space is established, the facilitator calls out an activity that each participant does. Thread a needle. Can you feel the metal of the needle? How thick is it?

How big is the eye? Can you hold the needle firmly? Can you feel the thread? How close to the end are you holding the thread? Is the end frayed? Do you need to wet the end? Is the thread too thick for the needle eye? Can you put the thread through the eye easily? Is the thread fraying each time you try to put it through the eye? Is the thread through the eye? How long is the thread? Bring the ends of the thread together. Knot the thread. Hold a rubber ball. How big is it? What is its texture? color? weight? Now bounce the ball. How high does it bounce? Do you feel the pressure as the ball bounces into your hand?—as you bounce it again? Now play a "My name is . . ." with the bouncing ball. Add speech as if you were playing alone but speaking aloud. Now let speech include at least one other person who is standing nearby watching you take your turn. Other possibilities might be: Put on a turtleneck sweater. Play hopscotch. Brush your teeth.

Systems Evaluation: Again, concentration is being taken a step further, into the arena on an independent basis but supported by the "cover" of the group. Security is gained by the tacit knowledge that everyone is involved in a similar task. Individuals feel the group's unified effort. By getting up and into the playing area, the student is working out into a life space. When speech is added, it is a natural outgrowth and natural expression of the activity. It helps *to show, not to tell about* showing; it helps demonstrate behavior and not talking about behavior. Personal security and faith should be accruing.

GAME FOUR

**Desired
Outcome:**   To discover the positive, concrete results possible from focused group concentration and participation with possible contribution of speech.

**Rules of
the Game:**   1. Group decides on size of playing field; rope holders.
2. Group concentrates until rope is clearly established.
3. Concentration holds on the actual playing of the game.
4. Group decides on the design of individual and multiple participation in rope jumping, on the "who" and "what."
5. Speech emerges, when used, from what is happening in the game.

6. Side coaching guides the game when concentration slips and unit participation falters.
7. Be willing to proceed. Build group participation.

Sample Game: Jump Rope

The class of thirty counts off in three. Three groups of ten each are formed. As one group plays the game, the other two groups watch from their seats. Two members of Group One pick up an imaginary rope in the playing field. They move an appropriate distance from each other according to how long they decide the rope is. At a given cue, "Begin!" or "Curtain!" from one member of the group, they begin to turn the rope. The two rope turners concentrate on each other's eyes to keep coordination in the turning. The rest of the students in Group One line up to jump rope. At a given signal from a group member, spontaneously decided, the first person in line concentrates on seeing the rope, jumps in and jumps rope. He jumps an appointed number of times and jumps out; each group member, in turn, jumps rope. When everyone has had a chance, the first jumper goes again and is, perhaps, joined by the second; they jump out together. The group decides, spontaneously, what combinations they want. Speech may be used as it comes spontaneously in reaction to the game. Appropriately singing may occur. If the rope turners tire, two other group members may take over control of the rope. After Group One has played a reasonable amount of time, they sit, and Group Two plays the same game. All three groups participate as doers and viewers before any evaluation.

Systems Evaluation: Only developed concentration from individual discipline can lead to group concentration that creates, controls, and plays the rope game. Side coaching should be used to ask the rope holders: Can you feel the rope? Are you turning it together? Are you turning too slowly for the jumpers? Do you want them to jump faster? The jumpers should be asked: Are you watching the rope? Are you stepping on the rope? Is your body responding to the rhythm of the game? When the group concentration is at its best, the rope becomes a tangible, evident property. When concentration breaks and group cooperation falters, the mental and muscular coordination of the group disintegrates. Note that by using the arbitrary device of numbering off to form the three groups, division is made quickly and easily, and the embarrassment of students being chosen by appointed group leaders according to previously established prejudices is avoided. The arbitrary division also allows for individual roles to emerge from the group's choice and activity.

By moving from the individual concentration exercises ("Directions") into the group activity, the student takes his growing faith and applies it to trust in others and in group cooperation. Each member must almost breathe with the other group members if the game is to succeed. Group discussion and evaluation following the third group's game should highlight group behavior manifested when concentration seemed at its greatest. Individuals should comment on how the level of concentration on the activity promoted a sense of group identity. The verbal language evoked from the game might also deserve comment. Concentrate; build group faith and trust. Discover how others behave in a group endeavor.

GAME FIVE

**Desired
Outcome:**   To discover how group concentration and participation can achieve a concrete, recognizable goal.

**Rules of
the Game:**
1. Establish concentrated silence.
2. Concretely establish the "where" of the playing field.
3. Determine "who" or "what" you are in this "where."
4. Work for group participation and cooperative participation.
5. If speech emerges from the "what," let the spoken language reflect an organic element of the game.
6. Be willing to proceed, to hold concentration.
7. Let concentration employ sensory awareness. Listen for needed side coaching.
8. Work for clarity, simplicity. Show, don't tell.

Sample Game: Join in the Activity

The class, the communication system, sits silently contemplating the playing field, the microcosmic arena of life. Each person is thinking of an activity that he can begin and that, when others in the group observe the activity, can join. When a group member decides, he goes into the field and begins. No one should join until he is sure, from what is shown physically without verbalization, that he knows the activity and can contribute. Possible activities might be: painting a fence; picking apples from a tree; weeding a garden. The activity should be confined to one particular kind of physicalization (painting, weeding, apple picking) so that everyone can participate and cooperate in completing one job. Side coaching should endeavor to help the nonverbal participants understand their limits. Painters might be asked: What are you holding? How heavy is it? How wide is it? What kind of substance is on it? Is the substance easy to apply? How high is the object on which you are working? How is that object constructed? Is it solidly constructed? Is the topmost limit straightedged? Is it of a particular design? The activity should be allowed to continue as long as unified concentration holds and until the activity seems reasonably complete. Verbalization, if a natural development out of the physicalization, may be acceptable. But the spoken language should never tell what the activity is; it should develop organically to facilitate the showing, the doing.

Systems Evaluation: Once the activity or several such activities have been completed, the group should analyze how discoveries were made regarding identification of the activity. A participant readily evaluates the manner in which problems of size, weight, shape, texture, and even color were determined before he joined in the activity. Some members of the system who never joined the game may try to discover those aspects of the activity that confused or misled; they may never have discovered the activity. Indeed, some participants may have joined too hastily, before establishing the activity from definite aspects clarified in the problem. This game continues to stress pooled concentration, the need to be specific in behavior, and focuses the individual group member's attention on the completion of one mutual problem. They share a responsibility and work toward satisfaction in a job mutually understood and cooperatively achieved.

It is important at this point, as the games require formation of groups and group decision, to strive for *clarity and simplicity*. By trusting growing concentration abilities and by having continuing faith in the action and interaction in the group, the game will develop through regular, meaningful discoveries. The communicator should behave simply, attempting to show through his spontaneous related action and reaction how human beings come together and solve problems with genuine satisfaction in the results. Simplicity is foremost—and difficult to achieve in a self-conscious, competitive world.

GAME SIX

**Desired
Outcome:**   To discover how a group member can contribute
                             meaningfully and in appropriate proportion with a
                             specific task to a group goal.

**Rules of
the Game:**

1. Determine "where" clearly. Define it physically. Maintain the physical restrictions.
2. Decide "who" you are and "what" you are doing there. From the behavior of other group members know "why" you are there. Once you join, maintain your role.
3. If speech emerges, allow it to develop from the situation and the needs of the relationship. Don't plan speeches; don't feel an obligation to speak.
4. Be willing to assume your natural role in a mutual experience.
5. Be willing to proceed. Have faith in concentration and participation of other group members.
6. Listen to side coaching for guidance.

Sample Game: Join in the Activity with a Relationship

The class, seated, confronts the playing field. After considering a simple activity that could stimulate others to participate in a growing, naturally evolving situation, one systems participant begins. Perhaps a student goes into the space, picks up an imagined broom, and begins sweeping the floor. Once his simple action is clear and a definite area is defined, a second person joins to enlarge the situation with a definite relationship; perhaps the student enters the space and begins to clear a table, as if a meal has just been completed. We then have the beginning of a situation and actions defining a possible place. If spoken language emerges spontaneously, it should be encouraged. But the student must not come into the scene with planned dialogue to *tell* the situation, his relationship, and the place. The dialogue should grow out of the activity and the relationship—mother-son, sister-brother, two daughters, or whatever—that the second communicator brought into the field. Once the actions and the relationship of the two seem clear, a third member of the system might join the game at the sink to wash the dishes from the cleared table; as this third relationship is integrated, another class member may join as the dish dryer, with a particular relationship in the family or whatever group has been established as occupying this now-defined kitchen. Each participant, however many join, must maintain his activity to its logical conclusion; the participants should be encouraged to relate verbally but not to "write dialogue." Side coaching to clarify the actions and the simple specifics of the physicalizations should be provided by the facilitator as required. Variations might be: Once the simple, organic relationship activity is accomplished and exercised, the students may benefit by taking the concrete situation into a more abstract realm. A student may move into the playing field and physicalize a tree swaying in a stormy wind. Students may join in appropriate order so that the final composite may include a forest of trees, a fugitive stricken with fear and running for freedom while being pursued by determined police and bloodhounds. All elements of the situation are appropriately represented by the human participants. The situations may become more metaphoric —perhaps more profound?—as the skill of participation increases to reflect group sharing of mutual concerns.

Systems Evaluation: With this game the student begins to determine, through simple, spontaneous activity, how human relationships are formed and how they progress under a given set of circumstances. Concentration continues to be crucial. Definite physical and situational limits are set. Within these the human being proceeds to determine his appropriate place in a certain group structure, in his limited "society." The student observers, the perceptive and developing "audience," should evaluate the game, using as criteria the truth of the relationships and of the behavior within the developing situation. Did the communicators trust their relationships and concentrate on the unified activity to simulate reality and truth?

GAME SEVEN

**Desired
Outcome:**   To discover how meaningful human relationships develop through spontaneous, concentrated verbal and physical cues.

**Rules of
the Game:**   1. Determine playing field.
2. Work for spontaneous response, verbal and physical, through concentration on partner and his behavior.
3. Trust responses. Let the situation grow.
4. Be willing to proceed. Let "who," "where," "what," "why," and "when" develop spontaneously.

Sample Game: Please-No

Two participants enter the playing field, and the rest of the system observes from the semicircle of seats. One of the participants must approach the other spontaneously, say "Please," and touch the second participant. The second person must respond "No" as a spontaneously uttered reply to the intention of the initial "Please" and move to another area of the playing field. The first person then goes to the second, says "Please" again—this time altering the intention in relation to the second person's first response; upon saying this "Please," he must touch the receiver in another spot. The second person must reply with an appropriately spontaneous "No" and move again; he may move to any area and use any level of physical relating: sitting, kneeling, lying down, or whatever is possible. The game proceeds until the "scene" reaches a point of appropriate conclusion as sensed by the group. Possible variations might be: Substitute nonsense syllables for "Please" and "No." Try "slidge" and "gruntch." Rely on the attitude projected through the voice to carry the burden of meaning; or use numbers, perhaps "one" and "two." Try abandoning sound entirely and substitute physicalizations for the words "Please" and "No." Work to express meaning through facial expression, bodily movement, and the unifying behavior between the two participating beings. It is always useful for the two participants to switch "roles" and repeat the game immediately.

Systems Evaluation: State the meaning of the scenes represented and analyze the manner in which the statements were made through use of word, voice, and physical movement. Consider the participants' projection of purpose in simulating a real situation of conflict in which this group of two was unable to reach a mutually agreed-upon solution. Try to discover when the encounter was most intimate, most personal; when the scene was most impartial and unemotionally involved. Let the participants comment on the way the human relationship developed and their reactions to pressures within the growing situation. Had previous work with establishing concentration helped them understand the human condition in which they were involved? Did sense-memory games provide an availability of perception appropriate to this stressful situation? Was it possible, under the conditions that developed within the dyad, to discover another way to solve the intrinsic human problem that was being demonstrated? Did the participants respond to the "Please-No" game as a simulation of a possible experience from life? What discoveries were made as the problem solving progressed?

Reminder: The participants in a communication system must recognize that games might have to be repeated many times, by new or the same participants, to clarify problems of concentration, spontaneity, faith in the participants' responses. All games must *show* the experience, not *tell* *about* the experience through inappropriate behavior and/or spoken language. If any of the games lose the immediacy of sharply remembered and applied sensory experience, the communication system, encouraged and coached by the facilitator, should redo the games that were mentioned earlier. Many facilitators begin all communication game experiences in class with a "warm-up" period of "Directions" or "Join in the Activity" to try to get the communicators in tune with one another, to vitalize the mutual life space that is growing with the help of communication games.

GAME EIGHT

Desired Outcome:	To discover how intense concentration and discipline can achieve human physical responses and involvement that virtually unite the behavior of two separate human beings.
Rules of the Game:	1. Concentrate on "who" and "where"; also establish "when," "what," and "why."
	2. Trust sensory responses that behavior motivates.
	3. Let any vocalization emerge from the solitary, private moment being experienced.
	4. Reflect, don't imitate.
	5. Try to let imagination proceed without inhibition.
	6. Maintain concentration through disciplined eye contact.
Sample Game:	Mirror Game

This game, like the sensory awareness game, is helpful to play early and regularly. Members of the class pair off. Each pair moves into the playing field and establishes itself so that there is sufficient surrounding space to avoid discomfort and possible distraction. In the groups of two one decides to act as the person looking into the mirror, the other as the mirror reflection. The person using the mirror may manifest any behavior. The two communicators should make direct eye contact and hold concentration through uninterrupted eye contact as all the behavior occurs. At the beginning, at least, relatively slow movement should be encouraged. The stronger the concentration, the more completely the mirrored behavior will become as one. The person instigating the behavior may choose a wide variety of behavior: combing hair, applying make-up, examining an eye that feels as if it has something in it, examining teeth and gums for food particles, getting dressed in a manner that requires contact with a mirror. The greater the imagination and creativity the more useful the activity becomes. The instigator might start exploring a small area and work to enlarge. If some class members stay seated to observe and analyze the behavior, they should work to understand how concentration through eye contact control leads to mirrored behavior that almost anticipates another's behavior accurately. If the observers have not been told who is the mirror image, the success of the game is measured by the difficulty the observer has in determining the mirror. After a reasonable time has passed, the participants should switch roles; the mirror becomes the mirrored.

Systems Evaluation: In this game intense concentration leads the players to a virtual union of motivation and behavior; the mirror grows to understand the intention of his source and is instantly responsive. The participants should comment on the contrast of use of concentration in the two separate roles, as mirror and as the person mirrored. The communicators should analyze how intensification of concentration affected awareness of self and nature of personal identity. If self-consciousness creates chattering and giggling at the outset, the group might analyze the manner in which the unrelated, embarrassed vocalizations dissipated and disappeared as concentration on the game increased. The intense "sound" of concentration should be recognized. Throughout the game the facilitator should coach as needed: Are you keeping eye contact? Are you an image or an imitator? Are you reflecting posture? All parts of the body? If the mirror game can be refined, a communicator will recognize the degree to which he can make nonverbal contact with another person.

GAME NINE

**Desired
Outcome:**   To discover how human relationships between two (closely associated) human beings are dependent on and develop through individual and mutual needs and motives.

**Rules of
the Game:**   1. Establish "where" concretely; establish "who."
2. Let behavior in environment reflect "when" and "what."
3. Let spoken language emerge from relationships and behavior within the situation.

4. Trust responses. Let the situation grow. Be willing to proceed.

5. Hold concentration. Listen and trust your intention.

Sample Game: Situation with Hidden Intention

This game has the structure of an improvisation. The situation is set up by the facilitator-teacher. Two or more students participate in a scene, and although they seem to be participating with similar motivations, each is attempting to direct the situation according to his own unexpressed intention. For example: A "mother," a girl student, enters the playing field. She works silently to establish her environment, a kitchen. After clearing the table, stacking the dishes on the sink, putting away uneaten food, and wiping the table top, she begins to wash the dishes at the sink. Throughout all this behavior she is obviously distracted by a thought that is plaguing her; she is obviously disturbed. The student playing the mother has been told by the class facilitator that she has introduced her daughter, Carol, a student in a local college, to a friend's son, Paul, also a student. The relationship developed, and the mother expects the couple will marry. Until this time the mother has strongly promoted the romance. The mother has just received a confidential call from a reliable friend who has discovered that Paul is a severe narcotics addict. The mother feels responsible for the relationship from its inception and is pondering the problem in an effort to find a way to get her daughter to sever the relationship without divulging knowledge of Paul's addiction. At this point Carol unexpectedly enters. She begins to wipe the dishes. She, too, seems preoccupied. The student representing Carol has been told by the facilitator essentially the same information the "mother" has had up to and including the fact that the Carol-Paul relationship seems to be leading toward marriage. But from that point on Carol has contrasting information and intentions. Although she has been devoted to Paul, she has worried about his lack of funds, because his family provides money and he works part-time with good pay. She has confided in no one. She has just discovered that his money is used to support a narcotics habit. Despite her strong desire to help Paul she has decided to break the relationship. However, she doesn't want to divulge Paul's secret to her mother, whom Carol believes still respects and admires Paul. The situation proceeds with the conversation developing out of each person's hidden intention, as each person attempts to steer the discussion in terms of what she *thinks* the other believes and knows about Paul. The scene progresses on the basis of what these two people say to each other and what they discover as they proceed. The class, listening, has not been told any of the information that the girls have received separately. The class must work to determine who these people are, where they are, what their concerns are, and, ultimately what are the hidden intentions.

Systems Evaluation: The "mother," through applied concentration and specific behavior, should have established the environment clearly. The mother's problem should have been suggested by nonverbal cues: her preoccupation; her rate of movement as related to the physical job that needed to be done; the relationship of her internal thinking—her internal monologue—to her tasks. Through all her preoccupation the mother must continue her physical activity. Similarly, the daughter's physical behavior —the dish drying—should be analyzed in terms of what unspoken meaning it projected to the observer. The listeners as well as the participants should analyze the development and nature of the dialogue; what they said to each other and why. The observers should work through the situation represented, interpreting behavior, action and interaction, in an effort to grasp the hidden intention. If the intentions were revealed at the end of the scene—the "game" the mother and daughter were playing— the believability of the revelations should be considered. If the intentions were not revealed and the class cannot discover them from the manifested behavior, these communication problems should be explored. This "situation with hidden intention" simulates the possible complexities that arise when assumptions and value judgments are assumed by members of a communication system, especially during a time of crisis. The problem of unclear human motive and the weighing of personal values complicate the system. The students, in simulated life experience of this sort, learn to explore in meaningful detail—through developed sensory awareness and focused concentration—vital aspects of their physical and emotional lives. Communicators discover more and more who they are, what they are, where they are, when experience occurs, and why.

GAME TEN

**Desired
Outcome:**   To discover how formalized behavior (for example, in literature) may represent, illuminate, and stimulate human behavior dictated by the communicator's background and feelings.

The classical literary forms of fairy tales and fables have been found to be extremely useful in classroom simulations. Although the popular notion might provoke a suspicion of "cuteness" or preciosity at the mere suggestion of the literary genre for the modern classroom, the literary form as written (see Grimm; Aesop) is terse, well-organized, unsentimental, and surprisingly applicable to personal relationships today. Furthermore, such literature covers so much narrative ground with clearly drawn characters so quickly that possible scenes, omitted by the author but logical and useful for students encountering and analyzing human behavior and interaction, are abundant.

Rules of
the Game: 1. Read the selection and clarify all pertinent facts. Don't depend on commonly sentimentalized versions of the selection.
2. Mutually agree on the physical setup (the ground plan) of the playing field for clarity of movement.
3. Concentrate on "who" you are, "where" you have come from, "where" you are, "what" you are doing, "why" you are here and behaving in this manner.
4. From the "curtain" let spoken behavior grow from the experience.
5. Have faith in your intention. Listen and respond as spontaneously as possible. Concentrate on the human relationship that is growing and the series of discoveries occurring.
6. Let your sensory responses work for the person you are representing.
7. Trust responses. Let the situation grow. Be willing to proceed. Hold concentration. Listen.

Sample Game: Hidden Intention Applied to Literature

Choose a selection of literature that concerns itself with behavior of people appropriate to students' lives. At a critical point in the narrative where the author has not provided a scene, but where one is possible, logical, and faithful to the author's intention, play the omitted scene. For example: In the fairy tale "Snow White and the Seven Dwarfs" the mirror has told the Queen that "Snow White fairer is she than you." Infuriated, the Queen considers action:

> At last she sent for a huntsman and said, "Take the child out into the woods, so that I may set eyes on her no more. You must put her to death and bring me her heart for a token."
> The huntsman consented and led her away. But when he drew his cutlass to pierce Snow White's innocent heart, she began to weep and say, "Oh, dear huntsman, do not take my life. I will go away into the wildwood and never come home again."

And as she was so lovely the huntsman had pity on her and said, "Away with you then, poor child."

He thought the wild animals would be sure to devour her, and it was as if a stone had been rolled away from his heart when he was spared putting her to death.[4]

Play the scene as Snow White and the huntsman enter the part of the woods before the cutlass is drawn. Snow White believes this man is her friend taking her for a walk; the huntsman's hidden intention is given, but his personal attitude toward his accepted obligation can be explored in his treatment of and conversation with the child before he acts. Would the huntsman confront the child face to face? Would he try to occupy her in a game and surprise her in murder? What manifested intention would he use to woo Snow White's confidence in order to pursue his hidden intention?

Systems Evaluation: The value of the fairy tale to communication games is the basically unsentimental, realistic approach to the fantasy. The narrative in its brevity and scope provides for creative yet logical exploration. The simulation of a premeditated violent act on an unsuspecting innocent allows the participants and the observers to explore motivation and behavior under such a possible circumstance. The participants must establish the environment of the encounter carefully; the "huntsman" must work to manipulate the innocence of the child in a situation that would facilitate the murder of that innocent. "Snow White" might work to help us understand the child's uncomplicated point of view. To extend the usefulness of the scene to have the communicators participating as well as watching, understand how the huntsman decided to free Snow White. "Please-No" might be used with the child using "Please" and the huntsman using "No," until the huntsman is no longer able to deny the child her freedom. Although the structure of the game represents an unwritten scene in a fairy tale, the simulation resembles incidents that we read about in our newspapers daily and must try to understand. As an extension of this game, the student communicator might be encouraged to write a soliloquy to probe the thoughts of a character caught in a dilemma. In "Rumpelstiltskin" the King has locked the miller's daughter in the chamber filled with straw with orders to spin the straw into gold:

There sat the unfortunate miller's daughter, and for the life of her did not know what to do. She had not the least idea how to spin straw into gold, and she became more and more distressed until at last she began to

---

[4] "Snow White and the Seven Dwarfs," *Grimms' Fairy Tales* (New York: Grosset & Dunlap, 1945), p. 167.

weep. Then all at once the door sprang open, and in stepped a little
man. . . .[5]

Write the soliloquy of "the unfortunate miller's daughter" as she sat there
trying to fulfill the promises of a braggart father at the risk of her own
life. Can a student enlarge his own perceptual field by simulating the
reactions of a girl, whose mother is dead, or at least absent, at the mercy
of two such men? Or look again at "Richard Cory" in Chapter 5 (p. 72–
73). Edwin Arlington Robinson gives the town's view of the revered citizen.
Try writing the soliloquy that Richard Cory might have spoken "one calm
night" as he "went home" before he "put a bullet through his head." The
poem is devoted to the town's perception. Try expressing Richard Cory's
perceptions and reactions that preceded his ultimate decision. Expand to
other types of literature as, for example, the first chapter of F. Scott
Fitzgerald's *The Great Gatsby,* in which Nick, the narrator, relates a visit
to Tom and Daisy Buchanan:

> . . . Daisy was my second cousin once removed, and I'd known Tom in
> college. . . . Her husband [Tom], among various physical accomplish-
> ments, had been one of the most powerful ends that ever played football
> at New Haven—a national figure in a way, one of those men who reach
> such an acute limited excellence at twenty-one that everything afterwards
> savors of anticlimax. . . .
>
> Why they came East I don't know. They had spent a year in France
> for no particular reason and then drifted here and there unrestfully. . . .
> This was a permanent move, said Daisy over the telephone, but I didn't
> believe it—I had no insight into Daisy's heart, but I felt that Tom would
> drift on forever seeking, a little wistfully, for the dramatic turbulence of
> some irrecoverable football game.
>
> And so it happened that on a warm windy evening I drove over to East
> Egg to see two old friends whom I scarcely knew at all. . . . Tom
> Buchanan in riding clothes was standing with his legs apart on the front
> porch.
>
> He had changed since his New Haven years. Now he was a sturdy
> straw-haired man of thirty with a rather hard mouth and a supercilious
> manner. Two shining arrogant eyes had established dominance over his
> face and gave him the appearance of always leaning aggressively forward.
> Not even the effeminate swank of his riding clothes could hide the
> enormous power of that body—he seemed to fill those glistening boots until
> he strained the top lacing, and you could see a great pack of muscle shift-

---

[5] *Ibid.,* p. 125.

ing when his shoulder moved under his thin coat. It was a body capable of enormous leverage—a cruel body.

His speaking voice, a gruff husky tenor, added to the impression of fractiousness he conveyed. There was a touch of paternal contempt in it, even toward people he liked—and there were men at New Haven who had hated his guts.

"Now, don't think my opinion on these matters is final," he seemed to say, "just because I'm stronger and more of a man than you are." We were in the same society, and while we were intimate I always had the impression that he approved of me and wanted me to like him with some harsh, defiant wistfulness of his own.

We talked for a few minutes on the sunny porch.[6]

Play the scene that takes place between Nick and Tom. Two volunteers from the class group play; if it seems more useful to the game's desired outcome, select the two players. Little if any consideration should be given to the physical description of the two men except as vital information to provide insight for the players in motivating the behavior of the characters being portrayed. The path to the porch and the porch constitute the playing field. Let the person portraying Nick begin by approaching the house and concentrating on establishing all appropriate aspects of character and environment. Nick's hidden intention, once the conversation begins, might be to discover if Tom really approved of him and liked him in college; Tom need not have a hidden intention. Or, if useful to the desired outcome, Tom's hidden intention might be to discover if Daisy, his wife, had explained, during her telephoned invitation, why the Buchanans had made this "permanent move" after drifting around the world for so long. An additional possibility might be: At an appropriate moment as the game develops, the leader might, through side coaching, call for a soliloquy (inner monologue) from either character. For example, as Nick approaches Tom at the beginning, the leader might say, "Tom's soliloquy"; perhaps at this point a soliloquy from Nick might be helpful in addition to or instead of Tom's. As the game proceeds and each player develops his intentions, overt and hidden, many such possible moments should emerge. Or such a soliloquy might be the most appropriate way to achieve closure before the leader calls "cut" to conclude the game. Similarly, investigate what possibilities exist in other excerpts from the same novel for the game "Hidden Intention Applied to Literature." Does the systems evaluation scheme for "Snow White" apply to *The Great Gatsby*? Might this game be used with such traditional sources as

[6] F. Scott Fitzgerald, *The Great Gatsby* (New York: Scribner, 1953), pp. 5–7.

A Tale of Two Cities and *Silas Marner* as well as more recent materials, such as J. D. Salinger's *The Catcher in the Rye,* John Knowles' *A Separate Peace,* Harper Lee's *To Kill a Mockingbird,* Philip Roth's *Goodbye, Columbus,* and Richard Wright's *Black Boy?*

OTHER GAMES

Once a communications system begins to explore and share the backgrounds of its participants and once those participants begin to build a mutual life space as a basis for meaningful communication in the present, the possibilities for communication games should emerge endlessly from the group. The games chosen as illustrations here have kept the communicators within the classroom while exploring their inner lives. At an appropriate moment, from our given communication system of thirty, nine students might go for a walk, if possible, outside the school building and return in half an hour. The group should cover the same general area, but the participants would agree not to make any spoken contact during the walk. The students should be encouraged to observe the environment fully: colors, shapes, textures, sounds. When the group returns, they should be given ample time to jot down all their remembered impressions of any kind. When this is completed, the nine students divide into groups of three and each individual reads to the other two their reactions. Once the three impressions are shared, the small group selects those reactions and impressions of the walk that seemed most common. Having chosen the shared experiences, the three members of each small group work together to represent their reactions in movement and sound. After working through the concept briefly together so that their pooled concentration is available and their intention mutually understood, each group presents the sound and movement improvisation to the class. The observers discuss the images and feelings evoked by the improvisations and evaluate, perhaps, in relation to the improvisers' intentions. This interpretative exercise in group reprocessing of a message may illuminate many aspects of nonverbal communication.

Another communication game that directly involves the student's environment might be called "Wrapping a Package." The student is given an appropriate amount of time, perhaps a week, to explore his home and to wrap an imaginative package employing materials readily available but not commonly used for the purpose. Commercial wrappings are not usable. The communicator may decide on the item that is being wrapped or the person for whom the package is intended and work on the wrapping accordingly. But the student should spend imagination and creativity. Nothing should be newly bought for the assignment and no needed item in the home confiscated. The participants might be encouraged to wrap an idea, a wish, a dream. On the assigned day the students bring in their packages and, in a mutually decided order, show the packages to the members of the class in a manner appropriate to the size of the package. Each student may describe how he wrapped the package. The class may ask questions. For each package the class guesses the intended contents. As each student finishes, his package is placed in the center of the semicircle formed by the students seated in their chairs. In evaluating the game the class should consider not only the imagination and creativity displayed but also the manner in which the students verbally explained the process and how the students handled—literally held in hand—their packages as they talked. What the human voices conveyed about the game should serve in making the evaluation. The students should also make an effort to consider the new form that is being constructed by all the members of the system as each new package is added to the growing collection on the floor. The game exercises and illuminates many aspects of individual and group verbal and nonverbal communication. This game was played by a group of thirty-three graduate students in a large, cosmopolitan university; one student, who at first seemed shy but grew to have faith enough to risk at least partial exposure in the communication system, motivated particular enthusiasm from the group with her package. The next day she handed in, unsolicited, the following:

Certainly

They were wrapped
   in thoughts
     and dreams
  long labored thoughts
    that lingered on
     a rainbow,
  paper clips, and a box
    of pain to be
     thrown away.

A pile grew
    creation upon creation
  like building blocks of time
 Each adding so much
    to the other.

Blues touched the soft
            silent greens
and yellows perched
            their mellowness
upon the blazing pinks.

Imaginations
                twirling
of hidden and spoken images
            of what had been
                    seen and
                            touched.

A pineapple emptying
                its golden candies
into our very souls
An elephant, silvery and gleaming
            looking proud on its
                pedestal of love.

In that pile upon the dirty
                floor
            I saw the world
Yes, the world—
        with all its cries of loneliness,
happiness,

                    laughter and despair
                    humourous and wasteful
                    angry and silent
The world *was*
            all there.

Can the whole world really
                be
        scattered randomly upon
                a concrete floor?

If you *let* yourself
                see,
        why,
            certainly!

                        Betty Glassman
                        July 15, 1969

By her own admission this student had written little if any poetry before. Whatever one judges the quality of this work to be, it clearly reflects an impressive personal response to meaningful contributions made to a communication system whose participants were creating an enviable mutual life space.

The following transcript represents an evaluation session in a graduate course, Creative Techniques for the Classroom Teacher, using games as an educational tool. The class of forty-one inner-city public school teachers, ranging from kindergarten through college, met once a week for three hours late in the afternoon. The group had one previous session in which "My Grandmother . . ." (Game One) and "Wrapping a Package" ("Other Games") had been played. This second session, with two students absent at the outset, began with "Directions" (Game Three) and "Self with Self" (the sensory awareness feeling Game Two). The students then moved out of their seats into the playing field and found enough space to block out through concentration the other people working in the vicinity. This was the first time the class was on its feet as a group. The leader/teacher/facilitator, Marge, then returned to "Directions," in the standing position, employing such sensory experiences as standing with eyes closed and concentrating on feeling the warmth of a midsummer sun on the individual's face. (The class is held in a windowless space, constructed as an amphitheater for lectures accommodating about 300.) After "Directions" Marge asked each student to find the person nearest to him; nineteen pairs proceeded to play the mirror game (Game Eight). After about ten minutes of the mirror game, side coached by Marge, the participants were, as expected, having varying success in holding concentration and "showing" rather than "telling." Several pairs, however, had established such intense concentration that the observers—Marge and Larry, a student who had arrived late—were unable to discover who was the mirror and who was being mirrored. One pair, Bob and Art, were so deeply involved that Marge, through side coaching, encouraged Bob and Art to continue but suggested that the rest of the class "cut" the game temporarily and turn to observe the pair. After five minutes of observation the partners were asked to resume their own mirror game. When Marge determined the game had achieved closure as concentration improved throughout the class—about twenty minutes after the students first found partners—she said "Cut" and the following discussion proceeded immediately upon the participants' return to their seats:

Marge (*the leader*):   O.K.—now what about this exercise? What did you really learn from Bob and Art? Did they achieve their goal? Who was the leader? The follower?

Sandra: They each seemed to have one eye in direct contact and the other eye watching the movement.

Jean (*who, during the exercise, took self-conscious poses in front of her "mirror"*): The main thing, they were watching each other's faces and not movement. I realized that what I was doing was concentrating on movement and not on my partner's face.

(*Bob and Arthur simultaneously raise their hands.*)

Bob: The crazy thing that happened—we suddenly realized there were moments when we ourselves didn't know who was leading and who was following. When you [Marge] said "Reverse roles," we almost had to freeze 'cause we really didn't know.

All (*a spontaneous group response of sudden discovery and approval*): Oh. . . .

Bob: We *really* were working as one.

Art: The funny thing was that we discovered this together but never stopped. But it was the eyes that telegraphed what was going to happen next.

Larry (*the latecomer who had observed the exercise and who, the first session the week before, had been the most resistant and vocally negative to the games and the concept of the games approach in the class*): You know when I came in, I knew something weird was happening. (*Burst of class laughter*) No—I mean good weird. The silence in the room was incredible. It was funny 'cause as I watched, it was almost as if the people were talking to each other.

Judy: You could *feel* the concentration!

Sara: Yes. When Marge said "Cut," we were all exhausted by a really good mutual experience.

Marge: What would you say we have achieved by now as a group? (*Many hands go up; some students begin to speak spontaneously. Marge calls on Tanza, an English-speaking student reared in Africa.*)

Tanza: It seems to me that you were trying to get us to realize we had to trust another person, our partner.

Marge (*obviously pleased with the response*): Yes—and who else did you have to trust?

Art: Ourselves.

Marge: Fine—and who else besides your partner and yourself?

Glenna: You—the leader.

Marge: O.K.—and besides your partner, yourself, and the leader?

Don: Well—we were trusting that everyone was concentrating on doing his own thing.

Marge: In other words, real concentration on the problem solving of the exercise was to work here as one with your partner within a larger group—it made you lose self-consciousness despite distracting influences all around you.

Larry (*the latecomer*): And you know it was beautiful—all beautiful to watch.

Marge: Yes—the one thing you [the participants] didn't have a chance to do was to watch each other. Larry and I could watch—but mainly it was *interaction* that was beautiful to watch.

Loretta (*about forty-five years old*): This was a terrific experience for us, but I teach very young children and would it work for them? Because their attention span is so short.

Marge: Remember what your own ability to concentrate was like at the beginning of this session when you all came from a full day of teaching?

Loretta: We were a tired wreck!

Marge: Exactly. The purpose of the exercise is to learn how to develop and lengthen ability to concentrate together. I have tried this with all age levels. I think you will find you are tempted to underestimate the exercises with children because when you approach a new area of experimentation in learning, you tend to underestimate the participants as well as the exercises.

Maurice: Well the exercise certainly reflected group spirit.

Bob: This kind of atmosphere we must try to establish when we break down into small groups—no matter what learning experience we're sharing.

Marge: Yes—consistently and continually no matter what we're doing.

What was observable in carry-over from the mirror game immediately was the group's spontaneous handling of discussion of the game; the group maintained a high level of concentration and relevant thinking and listening.

It cannot be stated strongly enough and reiterated too often that the material of this chapter is descriptive, illustrative of an approach to meaningful, shared experience in a communication system. It is *not* a plan, a formal scheme for learning. Let us reiterate: Specific, detailed, and extended treatment of the communication games approach might best be found in Grace Stanistreet's *teaching is a dialogue* and Viola Spolin's *Improvisation for the Theater*; perhaps no better guides exist. Viola Spolin, in her handbook's Orientation Sessions alone, provides enough germinal information for months—perhaps years—of creative and productive communication games. She moves from nonverbal to verbal games, from distilled sensory awareness games to complex group involvements. Perhaps Miss Spolin in discussing the "creative experience" makes the best case for considering communication games to facilitate group learning:

We learn through experience and experiencing, and no one teaches any-one anything. This is as true for the infant moving from kicking to crawl-ing to walking as it is for the scientist with his equations.

If the environment permits it, anyone can learn whatever he chooses to learn; and if the individual permits it, the environment will teach him everything it has to teach. . . .

Experiencing is penetration into the environment, total organ involve-ment with it. This means involvement on all levels: intellectual, physical, and intuitive. . . .

. . . When response to experience takes place at this intuitive level, when a person functions beyond a constructed intellectual plane, he is truly open for learning.

The intuitive can only respond in immediacy—right now. It comes bearing its gifts in the moment of spontaneity, the moment when we are freed to relate and act, involving ourselves in the moving, changing world around us.

Through spontaneity we are re-formed into ourselves. It creates an ex-plosion that for the moment frees us from handed-down frames of refer-ence, memory choked with old facts and information and undigested theories and techniques of other people's findings. Spontaneity is the moment of personal freedom when we are faced with a reality and see it, explore it and act accordingly. In this reality the bits and pieces of our-selves function as an organic whole. It is the time of discovery, of experi-encing of creative expression.[7]

[7] Spolin, *op. cit.*, pp. 3–4.

Nine

A Dialect for Meaning

In the traditional classroom students who have not spoken what has been labeled "standard American English" have been plagued by teachers and often coerced into acquiring certain prescribed dialectal patterns. These teachers seem to proceed on the premise that anyone who does not use standard American-English speech patterns is automatically doomed to a future of personal and professional failure. What these teachers may not realize is that the student may feel that disenfranchisement of his manner of speaking may imply rejection of his background and that, consequently, the student will place unconscious obstacles in the way of learning standard American-English speech.

LISTENING FOR DIALECTAL PATTERNS

The participants in a system working for communication clarification may discover that serious reconsideration and reevaluation of the communicators' *listening* habits may be the starting point. Traditionally, in the classroom oriented toward the proposition that there is only one "correct" way of speaking English, variant sounds and structures were not only labeled as "incorrect" but also discarded as intellectually and socially inferior. This attitude encourages judgmental listening, which is challenged by a more linguistically constituted approach to language learning. For its purposes and the practical considerations of life beyond the classroom, the communication system might decide to devote its energies

157

regarding dialect to training the listeners in decoding habits so that new dialectal patterns are recognized and understood at all levels. Thus an otherwise "closed culture" begins to adjust to its new participants. A communication system that chooses to retrain listening before deciding on the need for "new" dialects may be more open to discovering the manner in which variant dialects have influenced each other. As J. L. Dillard points out:

> . . . [T]here remains the very strong possibility that even the speech of American whites—and especially of Southerners (perhaps, ironically enough, even some of those Southerners who are most bitterly racist)—has been influenced by the speech of the Negro to a greater degree than historians of the language have been willing to admit. Charles Dickens, in his *American Notes,* expressed the theory of Negro influence on the speech of American whites as long ago as 1849, and a lot of ink has been spilled to prove that he and others like him are wrong. Unfortunately, the purely linguistic problem has been entangled with political problems and matters of race prejudice. Many linguists have in effect given up the study of Negro dialects because statements that some Negroes speak differently from whites can be taken to mean that they have "thick lips" or even "thick brains." But we have apparently reached the point where these absurdities need no longer stand in the way of serious research. When such research is completed, the picture of what went on in the history of American English may be changed a great deal. It may also be that English teaching will have to change.[1]

The system ready to listen attentively to the sounds and structures of its participants is conducting its own "research," as Dillard uses the term, thus formulating the group's attitude toward dialect adjustment and helping students to avoid what William A. Stewart calls "the sweeping . . . of Negro dialect descriptions under the white-oriented geographic rug. . . ."[2]

The teacher should recognize that the student has reached the level at which the teacher is encountering him, with a certain dialectal pattern; and the student may feel that he could perhaps succeed in the "outside" world with the same dialectal pattern. But what we have to offer the student is the availability of a second dialectal pattern that might be

---

[1] J. L. Dillard, "Negro Children's Dialect in the Inner City," *The Florida FL Reporter* (Fall 1967), not paginated.
[2] William A. Stewart, "Sociolinguistic Factors in the History of American Negro Dialects," *The Florida FL Reporter* (Spring 1967), not paginated.

useful to him if he moves out of his immediate environment. What we are in effect saying to the student is: "You are going to have to deal with a bigger world than you heretofore encountered. Another dialectal pattern might be more efficient and avoid possible stereotyping." An additional outcome might be the creation of knowledgeable acceptance of other dialectal patterns so that a voice that is itself stereotypic of a specific region (Brooklyn) would not be heard to say—as it actually was—"I hate black English. It sounds awful. It's so uncultured."

THE BLACK DIALECT

The black American now demanding rightful recognition—visibility—in a heretofore closed culture corporation provides particularly pertinent evidence here. Consider an actual communicator, Wallace, a black reared in as intensely restrictive an ethnic locale as any that exists in a large American city today. Wallace, of superior intelligence, is enrolled in a city university system for which he has qualified not by grades achieved in his public high school, which downgraded him, but through an experimental program designed for the so-called culturally deprived, the culturally disadvantaged student, in other words, mostly blacks and Puerto Ricans. Wallace is in a system of thirty-three students, of widely mixed ethnic, religious, economic, social, and political backgrounds; student ages range from sixteen to twenty-five. There are three other blacks, two Puerto Ricans, a Chinese, and those remaining are an assortment of whites. The course is called "Oral Communication." To begin to share his background so that the thirty-three communicators may begin to build their unique "culture," Wallace chooses to take whatever time might be available to him during the semester (determined as the group works together) to explore with the entire class his experiences as a heroin addict who has "kicked the habit" and is working to build a meaningful life. At one point during the first two weeks of a class meeting three times a week Wallace chooses to explain the "advantages" of drug addiction. Through reverse psychology he proceeds to enumerate the dangers of addiction as if they were—as they *are* to the addict—advantages.

But Wallace's speech is of particular concern here. For when he begins, although he is from the prototype of all black ghettos, there is virtually no trace of dialectal pattern. His processing of the message to this group at this point requires a clarity in denotation that he unconsciously reflects in what might be called a "standard" pattern. His facts are delivered vocally in such a manner that anyone, anywhere, who understands a reasonably educated level of spoken American English, would readily understand

and receive the message without sound distortion from the encoder. This extemporaneous delivery is *not* consciously controlled. Wallace's intelligence, ear, and intrinsic language facility are at work. Then Wallace suddenly turns to a member of the class sitting nearby and begins a conversation as if his classmate were also an addict and Wallace were looking for a "fix"; phonemes change, intonation alters to suggest more a regional restriction; grammar and vocabulary become so highly specific and colloquial that other class members are heard to whisper, "What did he say? What does that mean?" Again, Wallace is not consciously demonstrating speech facility. His speech patterns are affecting his behavior. This is not an *acted* performance. As the class begins to chat among themselves in an effort to clarify the confusion of the sudden change in Wallace's encoding behavior, Wallace suddenly stops talking to the individual student and turns on the class. With intensified utterance he vehemently says, "If you don wanna listen to this, get out—split!— And if you stay, man, shut up!"

Here Wallace is misreading the developing subsystems as inattention and rudeness on the part of the other students. This enrages him, and he uses the sounds that project rage in his ghetto—sounds varying sharply from those that the majority of the participants in that communication system would employ under similar circumstances. But probably no one else would have decoded the class' behavior as Wallace did—no one else was a black former narcotics addict encountering a relatively unfamiliar group, the majority of whom were prosperous whites. When he returned to his topic to summarize his remarks, his speech approximated what the group had heard when he began—but not entirely. Vestiges of the rage and, therefore, the sounds and structures used in that very personal rage, lingered. When the group analyzed the experience, Wallace recognized (if yet not entirely convinced) that he had misread feedback; the group contrasted the sounds that Wallace had uttered in relation to the kinds of sense his messages were carrying throughout his communication. What was of particular concern and, not surprisingly, remarkable to Wallace and the others was Wallace's utterance under personal pressure: His life style emerged. The communicators in the system, particularly the most conservative whites, were first loath but finally willing to admit that they were intimidated by a forceful, high-pitched sound that they associated now and for years with black threat. Wallace, however, indicated that he did not hear the change in sound under the stressful circumstance. He stated that in more relaxed, neighborhood circumstances, when "rapping" with friends, he sometimes was aware of similar sound differences used with less vocal vehemence.

Furthermore, as the discussion progressed through the hour and into subsequent class meeting hours, the threat component of the entire communication system decreased as the mutual life space widened, so that, finally, one white student had established enough trust to admit to Wallace that since Wallace's blackness was relatively "light" in actual color, he—the white student—thought he felt less threatened by Wallace's outburst than he might have been had Wallace been of a darker skin color. What emerged as particularly pertinent in this class in oral communication was whether Wallace's vocal behavior under stress—a kind of "foreignism" to the majority of the communicators in this particular system—needed conscious adjustment and practice to ensure clarity of denotative meaning, particularly in periods of stress, when connotative meaning, accumulated through untold years, is inevitable. Other members of the communication system had similar decisions to make regarding speech habits and needs for clarity in this classroom. A native American girl of Irish descent had absorbed an intonation pattern, natural to her Dublin-born mother, that suggested a supercilious attitude that the girl never intended; the Chinese student used an ostensibly foreign intonation pattern and substituted nonnative sounds when speaking on subjects reflecting his personal background but rarely when processing information of a more general nature. Essentially all the members of the class had to decide what speech habits worked most efficiently for the needs of the communications system in achieving clarity.

When Wallace acted as leader in a small group discussion of methadone treatment for heroin addicts later in the term, the efficiency of the vocal delivery in service to the intended meaning of the messages was a conscious concern, not only to those participating in the group, but also to those listening when the mutual experience of the discussion was subsequently analyzed. The entire system worked consistently to discover, analyze, and try to solve the problems that dialect in speech may provide even in the most intimate mutual experience. The small group, numbering six including Wallace, comprised communicators all of whom had dialectal variations, some of which were severe when the class first met. All members had decided what speech adjustments might be needed, if any. One boy, Murray, had a regionalism so strong that one member of the class originally thought he was a foreign student who spoke English as a second language. By the time the small group presented its findings concerning methadone treatment, Murray had managed, by identifying, clarifying, and practicing new patterns more useful to his needs, to process a stream of speech that was not identified as distracting and damaging to his intended denotative meaning.

THE CULTURAL REFLECTIONS OF LANGUAGE

Black—and yellow and Italian and Jewish and German—speech "for-eignisms" have provided connotative values in American society, values often based in ignorance and bigotry and leading to, seemingly, impene-trable barriers. Similarly, fear and threat have produced ill-founded linguistic conclusions. The difficult, but not impossible job, is to work to reach the denotative source of the language sounds, rhythms, structures, and vocabulary as they join to produce reasonable denotative meaning.

Our consideration of the classroom as a modern communication system has attempted thus far to establish the vast complexity of such a system when two or more participants of varying backgrounds attempt to find verbal and nonverbal meaning in it. In the systems described earlier, we have assumed that the communicators, in their attempt to build a life space based upon common experience in the classroom, are more or less representatives of the same "culture"; that is, "culture" defined as the "ways of people,"[3] as "structured systems of patterned behavior," as "the sum total of ways of living built up by a group of human beings, which is transmitted from one generation to another." Groups in and out of the classroom find strength in such identification. Indeed, the life space concept as developed in Chapter 2 suggests that a communication system is its own unique "culture": a confluence of all the communicators readily willing to expose their past lives, attempt investigation of their own back-grounds and those of their fellow communicators, and proceed with ever-expanding perception to experiment with, analyze, and, with concentra-tion, solve those problems that are of mutual concern to a developing communication system.

Robert Lado in *Linguistics Across Cultures* summarizes his concepts by stressing the manner in which language reflects cultures. Lado urges that we look closely at contrasting elements between and within cultures and work to understand how our verbal messages may or may not repre-sent these contrasts accurately. We must work to clarify and understand regular functional behavior of people within a culture ("cultural form"), the meanings ascribed to such behavior patterns ("cultural meaning"), and the patterns of distribution of this defined behavior within a given culture ("cultural distribution"). The more complex any one culture is, the more possible are the varieties of form, meaning, and distribution; it follows that the more numerous the separate cultures represented in a communication system are, the more intricate and variable is the process.

[3] Robert Lado, *Linguistics Across Cultures* (Ann Arbor: University of Michigan Press, 1957), pp. 110 ff.

And common code in a civilized communication system must work to serve the need of clarifying meaning, whatever the system's variant dialectal components.

Applied linguists, such as Joan C. Baratz and her colleagues at the Center for Applied Linguistics in Washington, D.C., are supplying descriptive materials that enable communicators who use standard American English to understand that black dialectal speakers (and, by extension, all dialectal speakers) also use "a well-ordered, highly structured, highly developed language system which in many aspects is different from standard English."[4] This linguistic research is based on three assumptions:

1. All human beings develop a structured language and no language is "superior" to any other.
2. Environment provides the context in which a child learns and develops his language.
3. A child has developed language by the time he is five; the necessary "rules of his linguistic environment" have been set.

Baratz contrasts standard American speech with nonstandard black dialect in respect to sound system, grammar, and vocabulary, the scheme followed in this chapter.

If we consider the approach of Lado and Baratz, the American cultural form "classroom" may have new meaning and distribution in the communication system of a public school classroom in urban America. However many native American cultural variants you may have envisioned as possible, add the Cuban exile's child or the Puerto Rican student who is one of twelve children in a family or the Hungarian teen-ager whose parents fled their native country in the revolution of 1956 and so on. What does the utterance "This is a classroom" mean to such a group when the group meets for the first time? What does the reader want this utterance to mean when the group meets for the last time—weeks, months, years later? The immediate concern here is the challenge faced by the classroom participants—teachers and students. Both must work to achieve clarity in messages—and, in particular, *spoken* messages—understandable for denotative purposes by all members of the system without denying the possibility and practicality of the existence within the classroom of smaller groups that maintain personal, perhaps more limiting speech habits. That is, how should we approach the problem of strong

[4] Joan C. Baratz, "Language and Cognitive Assessments of Negro Children: Assumptions and Research Needs," *ASHA* (American Speech and Hearing Association), (March 1969), p. 88.

speech dialect that occurs in the communication system—dialect introduced into the communication system from a foreign country or dialect
representing background and controls that may not be shared by the
majority of native American English speakers in the classroom?

A LINGUISTIC APPROACH TO UNDERSTANDING LANGUAGE

One answer to this question takes into account that the communicators—
preferably all participants in the system but especially the teacher—need
to identify and compare:

1. Meaningful *sounds* (phonemes) of the variant dialects represented in
   the classroom
2. The characteristic meaningful intonation patterns; that is, the characteristic rhythms of the dialects that carry meaning through established
   pitch patterns that provide a "stream of speech" in the spoken utterance in the classroom
3. The structural devices of the language—its characteristic grammar—
   that signal meaning for the system participants
4. The vocabulary that precisely serves the needs of meaning for the
   participating communicators.

Modern linguists have developed techniques that provide scientific methods for discovering and controlling these four elements within a communication system that chooses to change or control definite dialectal
variants within a given "culture."

As indicated earlier in this book, the attitude toward spoken language
in the classroom should not be one that aims at a rigid "correctness" to
which every so-called educated person must adhere for human approval
and acceptance. A human being's personal speech habits, his idiolect in
his native language, are generally a reasonable expression of his life's
experiences. They reflect his life style. Indeed, a marked dialect from a
ghetto dweller may reflect a lifetime—and a life style—of a more intense,
a more culturally rich constellation of experiences than that reflected by
the utterances of the more "standard" speaker in the communication
system. The ghetto dweller's language should not be misconstrued or
labeled by *any* member of the communication system as "incorrect."
Though the dialect of the ghetto dweller may be obscure to the student
who has had fewer limitations—social, economic, political, educational—
that dialect may be much more specifically descriptive and personally
meaningful than his own speech. The same principle holds for the

communicator whose native language is foreign to the system in which he is a participant. But whether the utterance is a dialect of American English, however variant, or a "foreign accent" resulting from influences of the language of another geographical region (Puerto Rico, Israel, Italy, or wherever), the approach to dialectal adjustment may be the same.

Remember that the communicator's *need* for dialectal control to meet efficiently and successfully the demands of those areas of life in which he chooses to be mobile dictates a communication system's attitude toward dialect adjustment; dialect is not "bad" or "good"; it has appropriate use within an established framework. The more varied the experiences of a communicator are, the more varied that communicator's input and processing of verbal and nonverbal messages may be when closely analyzed and evaluated.

Essentially, developed scientific techniques in the teaching of English as a foreign language are applicable and efficient in helping to establish a basis in *clarity* for life's needs in denotative oral communication. It is the responsibility of the classroom teacher—and not just in the foreign language classroom—to explore and apply these basic principles as needed.

The Carnegie Commission on March 3, 1970, published a report on "Equality in Higher Education"[5] that could not have made this need clearer. The commission's findings and subsequent recommendations considered the inequities in higher education due to economic and ethnic barriers. Precollege education was, of course, crucial. But, at all levels, the commission stresses particular skills that must be developed if, "by the year 2000, there should be no barriers to any individual achieving the occupational level which his talent warrants and which his interest leads him to seek."[6] On the premise that "the greatest asset of any nation is its people," the commission, with Clark Kerr as chairman, gave priority with the following statement:

> Because of academic and environmental factors associated with low socio-economic status, some students find it extremely difficult to develop the verbal skills that are required both for college entrance and for competition of college courses. Although academic success is also determined by mathematical skills, these, too, require verbal skills for proper development.
>
> The commission recommends the establishment of experimental programs for the early development of verbal skills, to be sponsored and

[5] *The New York Times,* March 3, 1970, p. 24.
[6] *Ibid.*

administered by institutions of higher education with active participation from members of the community; and of programs for remedying verbal skills deficiencies at the secondary and higher levels of education.[7]

The principles and attitudes already demonstrated in this book testify clearly to our endorsement of the commission's findings and recommendations; particularly, our responsibility to the verbal aspect of education, to what is here primarily regarded as the need for clarity in the spoken utterance. (The assumption is that language is actualized in speech before it achieves any other representation, if, indeed, language ever needs to achieve any other representation in a definite form within a given culture.) Rare is the classroom today, at any level, that does not include some variant, however minimal the representation, from a contrasting culture or subculture. In large urban areas ghettos produce communicators whose oral utterances provoke immediate attention. In addition, the native Japanese, Chinese, Italian, Israeli, Puerto Rican, Cuban, Hungarian, Greek, Mexican, and many other international representatives continue to enrich our country; the generations subsequent to the original immigration may continue to maintain certain dialectal influences due to restricted mobility and the language that persists within the home. The ghetto dweller—black, Jew, German, Scandinavian, or whatever—provides dialectal variation in the classroom toward which there must be a shared attitude in the communication system if it is to work toward a level of mutual clarity based on mutual need in communication. This should not be viewed as an effort to rob a communicator of his ethnic identification or the values, reflected in his speech, that he wishes to retain from his background. There is the desire to establish an understanding among communicators that where you are or where you are going (literally and figuratively) in your life may need to be considered, that there is a relation between mobility and the utterance spoken under given circumstances. Call it a "new language" if you will— if your native language is Spanish; if your western American dialect serves ranching near Dallas but not that executive position in Boston; if Williamsburg or Bedford-Stuyvesant in Brooklyn has provided habits in speech destructive to the intention of the American playwright whose work you wish to perform on stage in Chicago or read aloud in the classrooms of Spokane. The process, then, is to decide what habits a communicator wants to achieve and then to establish those habits. The process is not replacing but amplifying language experience. As the life space inside and outside the classroom enlarges and as backgrounds are

7 *Ibid.*

shared, students recognize the relevancies of fellow communicators' language patterns and grow to realize how certain habits serve more general needs.

CLARIFYING SOUND DIFFERENCES

To work meaningfully within a communication system, the participants, under optimum conditions, should first know the literal *sound* differences that exist between and among all the dialects present within the classroom. That is, each dialect has a particular phonemic structure: a structure of minimal utterances of sound that carry meaning. Figure 9–1 below indicates the mechanism involved in articulating the sounds of American English.

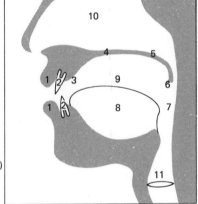

LEGEND:

1. Lips
2. Teeth
3. Gum Ridge
4. Hard Palate
5. Soft Palate (Velum)
6. Uvula
7. Pharynx
8. Tongue
9. Oral Cavity (Mouth)
10. Nasal Cavity
11. Larynx (Vocal folds)

Fig. 9–1

Not every dialect employs the same sounds or the same number of sounds, although most dialects share some sounds; but even these shared sounds may be produced by the speech mechanism in varying manner.

In the following list American-English consonants, vowels, and diphthongs are represented in words in initial, medial, and final position. Note the variant spelling (orthography) possible for the same English sound. For convenience, if not for use in a communication system where it may be judged by some as cumbersome, the phonetic representation of the sound is provided. The italics represent those written letters that may approximate in writing the sound that is produced in speaking.

Initial	Medial	Final	Symbols of the IPA
CONSONANTS			
*p*ea	re*p*eat	rea*p*	[p]
*b*e	re*b*el	eb*b*	[b]
*m*e	re*m*ain	Sa*m*, lam*b*, cal*m*	[m]
*f*ee, *ph*oneme	a*ff*air	cha*ff*, laug*h*, cal*f*	[f]
*v*enal	e*v*er	ha*v*e, sal*v*e	[v]
*w*e	a*w*ay	—	[w]
*t*ea	un*t*il	pass*ed*, pas*t*	[t]
*d*eep	rea*d*er	rea*d*	[d]
*n*eed, *kn*ead	de*n*y	dea*n*	[n]
*s*ee, *c*ircus	a*c*id, a*s*leep	a*c*e, las*s*	[s]
*z*oo	ha*z*y, rai*s*ing	bun*s*, buz*z*	[z]
*sh*ell, *Ch*icago	a*sh*ore	ra*sh*	[ʃ]
*Zs*a *Zs*a	a*z*ure, trea*s*ure	gara*g*e	[ʒ]
*ch*eese	a*ch*ieve	rea*ch*, (*ch*ur*ch*)	[tʃ]
*j*est, *g*erm	a*dj*ust	e*dge*, (*j*u*dge*)	[dʒ]
*th*ing	a*th*wart	ba*th*	[θ]
*th*at	brea*th*er	brea*the*	[ð]
*k*ill, *c*at	re*c*all (note the word "ax" is [æks])	wre*ck*	[k]
*g*o, *gh*ost	a*g*o	ago*g*	[g]
—	sin*k*, sin*g*ing	sin*g*	[ɔ]
*h*uman, *wh*o	be*h*avior	—	[h]
*wh*y	—	—	[hw] or [ʍ]
*y*ou	law*y*er	—	[j]
*l*eap	re*l*ieve, fi*ll*ed	rea*l*, sti*ll*	[l]
*r*eap	a*rr*ive	pea*r*	[r]
VOWELS			
*ea*t, *e*ven	b*ea*t, b*ee*t, bel*ie*ve, rec*ei*ve	s*ea*, s*ee*, L*eigh*	[i]
*i*t	b*i*t	pr*e*tty	[ɪ]
*a*te, *eigh*t	b*ai*t, b*a*te	s*ay*, conv*ey*, sl*eigh*	[e]
*e*ver	b*e*t	—	[ɛ]
*a*t	b*a*t	n*a* (colloquial)	[æ]
*o*tter	t*o*tter, c*a*lm	h*a*	[ɑ]
*aw*ful, *au*thor	m*o*re	p*aw*	[ɔ]
*oa*t, *o*ver	c*oa*t, s*o*da,	s*o*, s*ew*	[o]
—	w*oo*d, sh*ou*ld	—	[ʊ]

ooze, Uta	booze	zoo, clew, shoe	[u]
about	cut	llama, mocha	[ə] unstressed position
			[ʌ] stressed position
earn	burn	mother	[ɚ] unstressed position
			[ɝ] stressed position

DIPHTHONGS

ice	nice	high, tie, fly	[aɪ]
out	house	plow	[aʊ]
oil	toil	boy	[ɔɪ]
use	fuse	mew	[ju]

The sounds described here are those presumably used by that large percentage of the American population that speaks American English in our time in circumstances requiring clear, denotative, "educated" communication. Any major influence that could affect the articulation and pronunciation of millions might permanently alter the use of these sounds. With the possible exception of the initial sound in such words as "why," "which," "when," "whether"—more and more we use [w] instead of [hw]—little if any change in phoneme seems to have occurred recently despite the influences of world wars and social change in this country during this century. Certain regional sounds remain strong and reflective of a geographical dialect. Admittedly, subtle change through colloquial speech is an ongoing process. But there still seems to be an American sound made by professionals who dedicate their lives to oral communication in the spoken media that is recognized without argument as representative of nationally and internationally accepted sounds of American English.

With this basic introduction to the sound system of American English, the system that controls the spoken input and vocal processing of the American-English message, consider possible basic verbal problems that a class might face in determining the adjustment certain speakers might choose to make. In the black ghettos of the east coast of the United States one commonly hears the final sound in words like "mouth," "south," and "bath" pronounced as if it were the final sound in the word "half." That is, [f] is substituted for [θ]; the ghetto dweller influenced by years of particular pronunciation patterns may make the final sound in "mouthe" and "bathe" as if it were the final sound in "grave": substitution of [v] for [ð]. Joan Baratz provides further illustration:

> Although Negro nonstandard has many similar phonemes to those of standard English the distribution of these phonemes varies from standard English. For example /ɪ/ and /ɛ/ may not be distinguished before nasals [/n/,/m/,/ŋ/], so that a "pin" in Negro nonstandard may be either an instrument for writing a letter or something one uses to fasten a baby's diaper. Sounds such as /r/ and /l/ are distributed so that *cat* may mean that orange vegetable that one puts in salads—standard English *carrot*— as well as the four legged fuzzy animal, or a "big black dude." The reduction of /l/ and /r/ in many positions may create such homonyms as *toe* meaning a digit on the foot, or the church bell sound—standard English toll. Final clusters are reduced in Negro nonstandard so that *bowl* is used to describe either a vessel for cereal or a very brave soldier—standard English *bold*.[8]

Similarly, certain New York dialects, particularly those influenced by Italian, Russian, and Middle-European languages, pronounce the initial sound [ð] in words such as "this," "that," and "though" as if it were the [d] in the words "deem" "dam," and "dough." The final item ("though" and "dough") easily provides a distortion in meaning; the others may remain a dialectal distortion accepted on the speaker's terms, understood in context.

These random examples represent habits established through the influence of easily traced national influences of varying sorts. Even more dramatic in certain areas of the United States is the presence of Spanish speakers in abundance with varying facility in the speaking of English, further complicated by vastly varying control in the use of the native Spanish. English has many more vowels than spoken Spanish. But to complicate communication matters seriously, many of the consonants shared in isolation by English and Spanish may vary considerably according to the position (initial, medial, final) of the consonant in a Spanish word and, additionally, how the sound is used with other sounds. For example, English and Spanish share the sounds [s] and [p]. The close articulation of these sounds differs somewhat, but they are both phonemes in the two languages. In addition, these two sounds can be combined in both languages, as in the word "*es*pecial" [sp]. However, in Spanish, these two sounds never begin a word; they are always preceded by the vowel [ɛ]; in Spanish this combination of consonants is only

---

[8] Baratz, *op. cit.*, p. 88.

medial. In English as we know from the word "Spanish" itself, the two sounds can occur initially; they can also occur medially ("especial") and finally ("grasp"). The irony, of course, is that the sound of the cluster in English begins the word that represents the language in which the sound cluster is impossible: Spanish. The Spanish speaker learning English often struggles strenuously, sometimes with little success, to establish a habit that verbally produces [sp] initially without first providing [ɛ]. Even if all other sounds gain accuracy, the Spanish speaker may say, after much practice and adjustment of other variant sounds, "I e-speak e-Spanish" [ɑɪ ɛspik ɛspænɪʃ]. Such is the force of linguistic habit! If this were the only problem of this sort, the teacher might handle it easily with the aid of already established methods. But consonant clusters used initially in English words total thirty-nine; of these, Spanish shares only twelve—and this is only in the *initial* position.[9]

A DESCRIPTIVE APPROACH IN THE CLASSROOM

This brief illustration—superficial at best—is not to suggest that the communications system must become a class exclusively devoted to English as a foreign language in order to achieve genuine control of regional dialect and foreign accents within the system. It is to suggest that the facilitator in such a communication system must assume the basic responsibility for a scientific analysis approach so as to train meaningfully with available materials; through useful and tested procedures the teacher as facilitator can work toward a level of denotative competence that the participants of the system have decided they want to achieve. Whenever the communicators speak, *practice* is occurring—and can be controlled.

Furthermore, language and what it represents is a viable—an exciting!—area for small group as well as general system investigation. In attempting to discover what the components of the spoken element of verbal communication comprise, a communication system might well spend time enlarging its life space—in discovering ethnic, religious, national influences—by starting with a scientific evaluation and comparison of the sound systems of the dialects of the class members. Such investigation might uncover the influences these sound systems may have on the input, processing, output, and feedback potential within that verbal and nonverbal communication system. Small groups might then form around specific linguistic elements in the class, perhaps in an effort

[9] Charles C. Fries, *Teaching and Learning English as a Foreign Language* (Ann Arbor: University of Michigan Press, 1956), p. 17.

to probe cultural ramifications (ghetto life and its speech; inferences made by middle-class Americans when listening to speech marked by a Puerto Rican's characteristic sound substitutions; and others); or, more directly, small groups might be devoted to training actual dialect clarification with the guided help of the native speakers who seem to have the greatest control of efficient and "acceptable" patterns of native American English.

Recommendations in this chapter, as in the previous chapters describing possible teaching methods, are meant to be selectively descriptive of an approach; they are neither prescriptive nor complete. The intention here is to recognize the needs of a communication system and to stimulate participants in the modern classroom to seek further to fulfill such urgent needs. But here, as in the other communications areas, the students' consistent and controlled *practice* of the theoretical principles, with conscious analysis and evaluation, is of key importance to the success of the problem solving.

However the system chooses to deal with dialectal differences, the following examples serve to illustrate possible types of difficulties.

The vowel in the word "hot" is different from the vowel in the word "hat" (the phonetic transcription would be [hat] and [hæt]). If, say, a native Greek, Israeli, or Italian student or students with some English-speaking facility, participated in the American classroom, they might readily confuse these two words, since the vowel [a] as in "hot" exists in all three foreign languages; but the vowel [æ] as in "hat" exists in none of the three. If any of these students were to utter the sentence, "The hat is hot," distortion leading to possible misunderstanding despite contextual help in meaning might occur—the sentence might emerge sounding like "The hot is hot." The utterance might be further complicated by distortions in other variant sounds. This problem exists similarly, if not as dangerously, in regional speech of native speakers, particularly in vowel variants. More likely for regional speakers, however, would be the addition or omission of sound. For example, the pronunciation of the words "alms" and "arms" in certain eastern United States dialects may distort the initial vowel [a] in both words and omit the second sound in "arms" ([ɝ]—the first sound that occurs in such words as "irk" and "earth"). Both words, then, would be pronounced the same and meaning could be confused in the sentence, "His arms reached toward alms," which for the decoder might become, "His alms reached toward alms," due to regional dialect, although the meaning decoded in the particular region where [ɝ] is habitually omitted might be, "The arms reached toward arms." The native speaker may readily hear the difference between the two pronunciations and may be able to imitate the new pronunciation. Through repetition he may provide the desired habit.

On the other hand, even the native speaker may have difficulty in making the sound with muscles and nerves unaccustomed to working to provide this "foreign" sound. Furthermore, the student may not initially be able to hear the difference in contrasting sounds because of his hearing habits and relative acuity in denoting sound contrasts. The foreign communicator's challenge generally is more intense because the contrasting sounds (as in "hot" and "hat") may not exist anywhere in any dialect of his native spoken language. The Greek or Puerto Rican may easily *hear* the difference between "ship" and "sheep." But the vowel [ɪ] in "ship" does not exist anywhere in Spanish or Greek; the vowel [i] in "sheep" does. The foreign student may identify the difference when a native American says the sentences, "I took a ship to the United States" and "I took a sheep to the United States." But when asked to repeat the utterances, the Puerto Rican or Greek would more likely say for both, "I took a sheep to the United States." There may be other varying pronunciation distortions in the sentence, but only one will provide major meaning distortion: "sheep" for "ship." The neuromuscular pattern for a new sound [ɪ] may be quickly established; but, more likely, it may take much time, with patient and frequent repetition and listening in a controlled communication system atmosphere. But whether the communicator is a Greek exchange student learning American English or the Chinese ghetto dweller in Manhattan, the approach to clarification is essentially the same.

Admittedly, it may be naïve to believe that each member of the communication system, students and teacher, should know all the sound variants present within the given system. But it should not be naïve to assume that the facilitator, the teacher leading the system in symmetrical relationship, will have a working knowledge of all the major dialectal sound systems present in the classroom. The teacher who is in control of American English in its sound structure avoids guesswork and imprecise generalization that may lead to misunderstanding on even the denotative level. Today's teacher should know that in English, letters as written (the orthography of English) do not regularly represent the sound that is made; that there are twenty-six letters in the American-English alphabet but far more phonemes, the minimal units of meaningful sound. The teacher in control of denotative meaning in the communication system knows and hears these sounds and the problems that the participants in that system may be having with such sounds; furthermore, the teacher should know whether these sounds may occur in the same positions—initial, medial, final—in a dialect as they do in "standard" American English.

Comparison of sound systems is the first step toward clarification of dialect contrasts and difficulties. Once these differences are isolated, activities can be designed to benefit every level of dialect development in

the communication system: group speech project, reading aloud (a genuinely useful device in using another's material to exercise desired control
of established sounds for sense), and a wide assortment of communication games involving literal words as well as nonsense syllables containing sounds that would be of benefit for everyone in the system to use.
(For example, "Please-No" might be used with [na] and [la]; if the
dialect speaker unwittingly changes a "new" sound to one that is more
native, the system may discover whether meaning of the message in the
nonsense terminology changes despite absence of literal vocabulary.)

Let us repeat: A communication system working for clarification of
need in establishing a mutually desired verbal utterance pattern may
proceed inefficiently if a teacher does not know scientifically the technique of determining dialectal contrasts within the system; and how
practice—formal and informal, conscious and unconscious—to establish
habit must proceed to validate a mutual life space largely dependent on
verbal communication.

THE MUSIC OF DIALECTAL PATTERNS

Once the sound system of American English is established in the classroom, the communicators need to understand that the sounds connect to
form words that provide a characteristic stream of speech with characteristic intonation patterns; that a combination of established stress patterns
through recognized pitch usage establishes the meaningful "music of an
utterance." Every dialect has an intonation pattern that projects meaning
without the actual lexical items, without words that can be clarified
through dictionary definition. In a communication system containing
varying dialects, it is not uncommon to discover that what the listener
judged to be a foreign language being spoken was indeed the listener's
native language delivered with familiar words but an unfamiliar and
therefore bewildering intonation pattern; the music did not support the
meaning in American English. The native speaker of Cuban Spanish who
has "picked up" English—meaning, essentially, English vocabulary items
—generally utters a stream of speech marked vocally with Cuban Spanish
stress, certain variants in pronunciation, and overall rhythm that makes it
initially difficult to detect American English is being spoken at all. The
native of India who may have Indian English as his native utterance, may
sound, at least on first hearing, as if he were not speaking English: The
stress pattern intrudes upon American ears. Similarly the dwellers of
inner-city ghettos who have established specialized intonation patterns in
addition to highly specific vocabulary items, ironically enough, produce a
kind of American English that may sound foreign.

The task of the communication system, then, is to practice the language with enough monitored control, at least under certain given circumstances and allotted times, to guarantee that the sounds made and the intonations provided in connected speech make for shared denotative sense. Take the simple utterance:

This is a good movie.

As a direct American-English statement of denotative meaning, the previous figure, a descriptive linguistic technique, would suggest that all words preceding "movie" would be uttered at an optimum (usefully low and personally meaningful) pitch level; at "movie," to signal the imminent conclusion of the utterance, the pitch rises slightly at the beginning of the word and then drops to a conclusive pitch level lower than the optimum, the sustained pitch used for the four previous words of the simple utterance. This might also be represented in writing in this manner: This is a good MOVie. This is an American-English intonation pattern for a simple statement.

If a student in a communication system were from the island of Jamaica, for example, he may have learned English as his native language on the island; but the intonation pattern, affected by other influences, may not only vary the vowel and consonant pronunciation somewhat (without crucial meaning distortion) but also the intonation pattern. The change of music, however, might provide a new meaning for the native American listener, although the Jamaican's meaning with his characteristic intonation pattern might have the same intention. The Jamaican might say:

It is a good movie. (or: It is a GOOD movie.)

With vocal stress on "good," a stress achieved through rising pitch, the American might interpret the Jamaican as saying that this particular movie is "good" as opposed to one that is "bad"; the Jamaican's native habit—his ear and neuromuscular patterns—actually intended the same denotation without judgment as the native American's utterance. Here is different music for the same message—but the members of a given communication system, when that system has various and variant dialectal elements, must discover, analyze, and evaluate these differences scientifically. Then, once participants have decided to what degree the dialect speaker should work for adjustment to an American-English speaking pattern, monitored practice must be encouraged. The participants must assess the various personal and public associations that the communicator may encounter and, in particular, the linguistic necessities that must be shared within the communication system of the classroom for establishing as open and fertile a mutual life space as possible.

For final illustration of projection of meaning through dialectal intonation pattern, listen in your inner ear, if your experience allows, to the sound of the inner-city ghetto-reared black conversing intimately with friends in public—on a bus, walking to school, in a restaurant. One facet that emerges as dialectically remarkable is the extreme pitch rise that alters "American-English" intonation pattern above the levels usually identified in conversational ("white"?) utterance. (The American black may also employ a pitch *drop* rarely used by others.) In American English extremely high-pitch usage is usually restricted to situations of emergency or extreme, intense reaction (calling for help, expressing the supercilious); maintaining such a pitch is difficult vocally and may lead to laryngeal discomfort, since there is little consciously controlled breath support for this rare usage. But the ghetto black, in his most intimate moments when making his identity vital and culturally identifiable, as he has been forced to behave through restrictions of space, place, and relationship, vocally may employ a sound in English that few if any non-blacks use—or, more importantly, understand. The sound does not differ much from that made by the "soul" singer in flights of emotion through song; nor, we find, is the extraordinary pitch pattern unlike evidences of intonation patterns used in certain African dialects. Furthermore, the black can maintain this sound longer without strain: The pitch seems well supported. The black, just as every representative of an encompassing culture, has learned to adjust this vocal approach to some degree in relation to the nature of his participation in a particularized, yet more culturally heterogeneous communication system; it should be superfluous to point out that this happens regularly not only to the ghetto dweller with mobility beyond his ethnic or religious boundaries but also to the "average middle-class American" whose mobility may have narrower limits but who adjusts verbal and nonverbal behavior as his human contacts vary throughout a given amount of time within his personal life space.

WORD FORM AND WORD ORDER

The phonemes and intonation pattern—the meaningful sounds and the variation in pitch that provide characteristic rhythm—are but two of the four aspects of the spoken language that must be understood and controlled for meaning needs in the classroom. The remaining two are the grammatical structure and the existing vocabulary of American English or any language. As was discussed briefly in a previous chapter, the grammar of English has for years been handled in school by memorizing rules and identifying structures based on information perhaps pertinent to other languages but of little consequence to American English as spoken or written. The discussion of grammar can become intricate and, for our purposes here, overdetailed. But what the teacher/facilitator must recognize, even if the student communicators within the classroom never take the time to consider the theory of American-English grammar, is that the language, in practice, signals meaning according to the forms the words of the language take and the order in which those forms occur in a spoken or written utterance; that in American English, in contrast to, perhaps, all the other spoken languages of the world, meaning may change according to the position of the lexical item. Furthermore, the purpose of the utterance—to declare, to question, to demand—is also generally signaled by word order in addition to the use of specialized words. In ambiguous or particular circumstances meaning is clarified by the intonation pattern used if the utterance is spoken, or by the piece of punctuation employed, if the utterance is written. Consider the way meaning changes as the following spoken utterances are modified:[10]

Utterance	Meaning Change
1. The dog went away. The dogs went away.	The addition of sound in speech and the letter "s" in writing changed the number of items.
2. The dog is here. Is the dog here?	The words are pronounced the same in both utterances. For denotative meaning the word order makes one sentence a statement, the other a question.
3. The dog is here. The dog is here?	The word order in both are the same. In order to make the statement into a question, the intonation pattern would have a final pitch rise to denote question. In writing punctuation marks serve in place of the voice.
4. The dog sees the man. The man sees the dog.	The words in pronunciation and individual meaning remain the same. Only the word order change, when the doer becomes the receiver, signals meaning change.

[10] Lado, *op. cit.*, pp. 51 ff.

5. The man owns a dog house.
   The man owns a house dog.

The words in pronunciation and spelling remain the same. The word order changes meaning: The same word may be the thing modified or the modifier.

6. This machine harness . . .
   This machine harnesses . . .

The change at the end of a word by adding sounds [ɪz] alters the usage of the word (harness) and signals the structure that will follow.

7. The time of our lives that is gone . . .
   The time of our lives that are spent . . .

Correlation between two words in a structure signals the nature of subsequent material (time . . . is; lives . . . are).

8. Who is responsible?
   What is responsible?

Words with no lexical meaning signal a particular grammatical structure (here a question) and the anticipated answer. These words serve a function.

9. He sits on the chair.
   He sits by the chair.

A word with no lexical meaning serves the function of clarifying relationships of definable items in meaningful arrangement.

All of the previous, in the most simple available grammatical structure, serve as a basis for the nature of meaning as signaled through the spoken and written forms of standard American English. There are infinite varieties and amplifications; but those listed should serve as a basis for the understanding of structure—of word order—as the carrier of essential meaning in standard American English. It should be understood that even these simple units or partial units of meaning may vary when spoken according to the number of ways the voice can shift stress and thereby alter meaning. For example, notice the change in meaning that occurs as vocal stress, indicated below through capitalization, shifts in the following utterances:

> *in*put affects the processing of the spoken message.
> Input af*fects* the processing of the spoken message.
> Input affects *the* processing of the spoken message.
> Input affects the *pro*cessing of the spoken message.
> Input affects the processing of the *spok*en message.
> Input affects the processing of the spoken *message*.

A similar concept has been mentioned previously regarding the possible contrasting intonation patterns of native English speakers, from different locales (the island of Jamaica and America, for example), both wishing to denote the same meaning. Consider the possible complications when these speakers wish to denote contrasting meanings with the same word order and native intonation patterns that differ.

The following sign, in English and Spanish, appears in the subways of New York City. Comparison of the way the two languages deal with the same message illustrates the specific concerns a communication system should consider in working to understand and control dialectal variants in the classroom.

Warning	**Aviso**
Subway tracks are dangerous. If the train stops between stations stay inside.	La vía del tren subterráneo es peligrosa. Si el tren se para entre las estaciones quédese adentro.
Do <u>not</u> get out. Follow instructions of train crews or police.	No salga afuera. Siga las instrucciones de los operadores del tren o la policía.

Since this message is written and not spoken, the sound system and characteristic intonation patterns are not available for contrast. But linguistic analysis confirms that although the orthography of English is not equal to the phonemic representation (in subw*a*y, d*a*ngerous, tr*a*in the italicized orthography produces the same sound [e]), the orthography of Spanish is consistently equal to the sound representation. (L*a* vía, p*a*ra, and all other words with the letter "a" use the spoken sound [ɑ] to represent that letter.) The intonation pattern of the English utterance, as discussed earlier, remains standard unless additional signals are introduced, such as the underlining of "not." In speaking, a pitch rise and perhaps an increase in vocal intensity would provide a new pattern. The Spanish utterance has a more staccato delivery with regular stress throughout the utterance. Whenever word stress may be in question, a mark for syllable stress is used (never the case in written American English). In "quédese" the stress mark indicates that the pronunciation of the word has changed because the form and usage of the word has changed; that is, this imperative reconstructs the word, and the first syllable receives the stress.

The literal, word-by-word translation of the Spanish into English would read: "The way of the train subterranean is dangerous. If the train stops [more literally, stops itself] between the stations, remain [literally remain yourself] inside. [Literal translation is impossible with the next utterance. It would read something like "No leave outside."] Follow the instructions of the operators of the train or the police."

In Spanish there is no literal equivalent for "subway tracks," so the utterance becomes longer and more complicated, involving a modifier "subterraneo" following the word it modifies "tren," a structure rarely if ever used in spoken American English. The first sentence in English requires a plural verb "are," in Spanish a singular verb "es." In Spanish articles are used that signal gender ("La") and force agreement in form if the word is modified ("peligrosa"). This never occurs in modern English. The second sentence has the closest literal translation, with the difference being the Spanish use of the reflexive form of the verbs ("se para"; "quédese") and the required use of the article ("las"); reflexives are rare in English (for example, "He washed himself and then put himself to bed"), and article use is inconsistent, depending on intended meaning. ("The stations are conveniently located" may vary in meaning from "stations are conveniently located.") In the third sentence the Spanish imperative syntactic form places the negative first (which is perhaps the reason "No" is underlined only once), while in English "not," the second word in the sentence and a weaker word than "No," is underlined twice. The Spanish verb "salga" is an imperative form; in English the word order signals the imperative. In the final sentence again the imperative verb form immediately signals meaning ("Siga"), and the article "las" is added. But "train crews," which would include various personnel, is changed to "the operators of the train," a somewhat more specific though slightly distorted message.

There are other linguistic elements that vary, in the translation from English to Spanish, but these may serve as sufficient illustration to demonstrate the need for communicators to understand how both languages function if Spanish speakers in a system are working to acquire useful spoken English.

This contrastive analysis can be extended to an investigation of black nonstandard dialect and standard American English. Baratz provides the following selected illustrations using the syntax of low-income black children:

1. When you have a numerical quantifier such as 2, 7, 50, etc., you don't have to add the obligatory morphemes [the smallest form of a word that conveys specific meaning] for the plural:—*50 cent, 2 foot.*
2. The use of the possessive marker is different. For example, the standard English speaker says *John's cousin;* the nonstandard Negro speaker says *John cousin.* The possessive marked here by the contiguous relationship of John and cousin.
3. Conditional is expressed by word order change rather than by *if.* Standard English: *I asked if he wanted to go.* Negro nonstandard: *I aks did he want to go.*

4. The third person singular has no obligatory morphological ending in nonstandard so that *she works here* is expressed as *she work here* in Negro nonstandard.
5. Verb agreement differs so that one says *she have a bike, they was going.*
6. The use of the copula is not obligatory: *I going, he a bad boy.*
7. The rules for negation are different. The double negative is used. Standard English *I don't have any* becomes *I don't got none* in Negro nonstandard.
8. The use of ain't in expression of the past: Negro nonstandard present tense is *he don't go,* past tense is *he ain't go.*
9. The use of the *be* to express habitual action: *he working right now* as contrasted with *he be working every day.*[11]

ESTABLISHING A STANDARD

Clearly, the communication system whose participants have some facility in English but may vary considerably in regional and/or national dialects needs an agreed-upon "standard" for clarity in oral communication. Unless the class is devoted solely to clarification and adjustment of dialectal forms, it must be the responsibility of the teacher to determine the degree to which such conscious practice should proceed. But the entire communication system of the particular classroom should agree to cooperate in working to establish the appropriate level of clarity to fulfill immediate and subsequent needs. Oral practice is vital. The students with dialectal variants that distort meaning must establish more useful habits. Native speakers in the system whose patterns may act as models and who may serve as leaders in exercise should serve accordingly. Whatever approach seems most useful—small group projects, full class discussions, and drill—repetition of meaningful American English, with the "rules of the game" established by the communication system to meet the system's needs, must proceed. Whether the group and individual project is specifically to clarify language or is one in which language must be clear to serve intended meaning, everyone in the system should feel a responsibility toward the other participants in monitoring and maintaining the determined level of spoken American English. If a class has one of thirty communicators who is working to clarify an aspect of his vocal processing, the responsibility should be no less—though perhaps much less strenuous—than the communication system of thirty with fifteen or more communicators with severe variants in need of desired "new"

[11] Baratz, *op. cit.,* p. 89. Brackets are ours.

speech habits. Most important, of course, is the teacher's responsibility to discover and implement the scientific techniques to facilitate such an approach to dialect problems in the classroom. Each "foreign" language difference in the classroom, whatever the source, may require individual consideration for a complexity of reasons discovered when contrasting the students' habits with those established as useful for all members of the system. The job is intricate. The rules are definite. The process and ultimate results should be gratifying; the communicators will gain increased communication skills that should result in more meaningful human relationships.

The final formal aspect of language learning, which demands comment here, is the vocabulary of American English. With vocabulary, as with sound and structure, each language and each dialect within a language, may use what seems to be the most basic of lexical items—house, chair, bread, man—in a multiplicity of denotative and connotative ways. With vocabulary perhaps the most sensible approach is to take no usage for granted within the classroom. Certainly the teacher should understand, to a reasonable degree, the ways that words achieve and change meaning in a dynamic culture—particularly a culture undergoing obviously dynamic change. In the classroom students may use words that seem obvious in meaning but require amplification and examination. No communicator should hesitate to question another's use of a word, however common. Words that for years have maintained definite formal denotative meaning may suddenly achieve new widespread usage. The "hippie" community of the sixties used "bread" to mean "money"; when the urban black in the eastern United States introduced commonly used ghetto speech to the white community, it was discovered that the young black community used "bad," spoken in an intonation pattern indicating a definite positive attitude, to mean "good" in the sense of strong approval. Thus, a spoken sentence such as "That's a BAD tie" was a genuinely felt compliment to the wearer. Black children of the ghetto, enraged at each other and seeking the strongest insult, may shout, "You got a black mother." In this context the child uses denotation of his personal identity and reverses it to use as a literal obscenity. Similarly, the word "mother," with certain vocal delivery and in a particular context, becomes a vulgar epithet.

This is language at the colloquial level, but such language, when genuinely descriptive and useful, often quickly gains formal recognition. At this writing "rap" used as "meaningful, pertinent conversation" enjoys ever-increasing popularity with aware communicators in even the most "educated" environments. "Let's rap about student unrest" would, at this moment in 1971, confuse few if any aware speakers of American English. The word may disappear or lose currency quickly. But the communication system in search of accurate communication must recognize the language of the moment, just as it must feel a responsibility to check meaning of vocabulary items standard to American English. Students must always understand that other communicators in a particular system with variant dialects or foreign language components in their speech may confuse or misuse vocabulary items. Ask the necessary questions. Take time to clarify. And use intelligently prepared descriptive guides to language, such as the most current reliable dictionaries, which help to solve meaning problems. But whatever guides students use, the teacher in the communication system—even if no dialectal problems are judged to exist—should discover the materials available by eminent applied linguists. The Carnegie Commission, in its concept of the training of verbal skills as basic to its conclusions, considered the economic and racial imbalance in our schools. The commission's philosophy serves to summarize ours:

> The greatest single handicap the ethnic minorities face is their under-representation in the professions of the nation.
>
> . . . If a lack of ethnic self-awareness and a sense of inferiority begin in elementary school, then we must begin to attack these problems there.
>
> From kindergarten on, every student can benefit from learning the history of his own ethnic group; and those of his classmates, and about the rich diversity of his nation's culture. Such study is not a substitute for the development of basic verbal and mathematical skills, but students deserve the opportunity to study ethnic experiences and to use the intellectual resources of their schools to seek an understanding of problems of their own communities.
>
> All students, at every educational level, and with whatever vocational goal, must be made fully aware of the wide variety of backgrounds and values of their fellow citizens.
>
> By the year 2000, the commission believes that opportunities can and must be totally free of the last vestiges of limitations imposed by ethnic grouping, or geographic location, or age, or quality of prior schooling.[12]

[12] *The New York Times, op. cit.*

PHASE 4

THE OUTPUT:
Toward Perfecting the System

Getting Better

It's getting better all the time
I used to get mad at my school
the teachers who taught me weren't cool
Holding me down, turning me round
filling me up with your rules.
I've got to admit it's getting better
It's a little better all the time. . . .

THE BEATLES

Ten

A Learning Encounter

In the second chapter of this book five behavioral objectives were stated as central to the student in a communication-oriented classroom in which the teacher is functioning as facilitator of the system. If these objectives are fulfilled, the student will be able to:

1. Produce unique communications with emotional and intellectual content in an environment that is not threatening and allows for free interchange of ideas among peers and teachers
2. Play the role of the "second speaker" or the receiver of messages who listens willingly and responds with feedback that has meaningful intellectual and emotional content
3. Monitor his own communicative behavior and that of other speakers for analysis and evaluation
4. Control and improve his own communication and the operation of communication systems of which he is a part
5. Use his communication skills for solving problems and making decisions.

In the following transcript the teacher, Mr. Tharp, is attempting to fulfill these objectives. Analyze the success of the classroom encounter on the basis of the five objectives:

Communication System: Junior high school classroom in a ghetto school in the Bedford-Stuyvesant area of Brooklyn, New York

Communicators: A group of thirty-two students—seventeen blacks,
                            ten Puerto Ricans, five whites—and one teacher

Facilitator: White male, twenty-nine years old, native of large
                            Midwestern city where he was graduated from a
                            "big ten" university

*(Note that this class met for two hours without interruption for any cur-
ricular reason. It was interrupted, at about 11 A.M., for a fire drill.)*

Mr. Tharp: Remember the poem we read together and discussed yes-
             terday? (*Class nods and responds, "Yes."*) Remember the
             feelings we said we felt after hearing the poem? Paulette,
             would you read the poem again for us . . . and let's try to
             recall some of those feelings and ideas.

Paulette (*reading from a mimeographed sheet the class received the day
         before*):

What happens to a dream deferred?[1]

Does it dry up
like a raisin in the sun?

Or fester like a sore—
And then run?
Does it stink like rotten meat?
Or crust and sugar over—
like a syrupy sweet?

Maybe it just sags
like a heavy load.

Or does it explode?

Mr. Tharp: Thanks, Paulette.
Paulette: Oh—did everybody hear me today . . . 'cause yesterday
             Robert said he couldn't hear me the last time.
Robert: I heard you good this time. But when something explodes
             . . . like . . . that's big, like a ball.
Mr. Tharp: Is that the kind of explosion that happens in this *dream?*
Paulette: No.
Mr. Tharp: Then why do you think he uses those words? Words like
             "dry up" and "fester"?
Richard: I don't know, but I forgot what "deferred" means.
Paulette (*spontaneously*): Put off . . . not right now . . . maybe you can
             do it later, but you're not sure. . . .

[1] Langston Hughes, *The Panther and the Lash* (New York: Knopf, 1969), p. 84.
Reprinted by permission. Also reprinted by permission of Harold Ober Associates, Inc.

Richard:	Well all right. But gettin' back to those words about rotten meat. I don't really know . . . but when *I* dream, it don't stink.
Mr. Tharp:	Well, Richie, what *do* you dream about? . . .

(General laughter that builds in the part of the room where Richard is sitting)

Mr. Tharp:	How many of you remember dreaming?

(Hands begin to go up, some rather cautiously. Finally all but about seven hands are up.)

Mr. Tharp:	What about the others? Don't you . . . when you sleep . . . don't you remember something that you dreamt during the night?
Joseph (*who was one of the seven who did not raise his hand*):	Martin Luther King had a dream . . . we talked about it on his birthday. . . .
Mr. Tharp:	Yes . . . well try to remember some of the things we said and try to think about your own dreams . . . the ones you have while you sleep . . . or maybe you can think of dreams like Martin Luther King's if you didn't have a dream last night or the night before. Why don't we write about our dreams? (*To George*) You raised your hand, didn't you? (*George nods.*) You others? Okay?
Janet:	I haven't had no dreams. . . .
Mr. Tharp:	Night before last? Night before? Night before that? *(She shakes her head "No" through all these questions; the class giggles and breaks into general laughter.)* Okay. How about trying a dream like Martin Luther King's?
Janet:	Well . . . like . . . Okay, I guess I can try. . . .
Mr. Tharp:	Okay. Now. What I want you to do is simply to talk about the dreams in writing. Write a dream that you had . . . either the dream you had last night or the night before. Put it down as you remember it . . . or a dream you had last year . . . or, like Janet, perhaps something you imagined during the day: a daydream. And while you're writing, try to remember everything, even the feelings you had if you can remember your feelings during the dream. Let's see what we come up with . . . and then maybe you'll want to read your dreams to the class . . . some of you . . . all right? So could we try? Remember, if you need to, find a dream, like Martin Luther King. Everyone got paper and something to write with?

(A general noisy scramble until everyone gets necessary materials)

Mr. Tharp: Okay. Take it easy now, and let's try to get those dreams. *(The following interval of ten to fifteen minutes is generally quiet, reflecting the students' concentration on the work. When some noise occurs, usually due to a student's finishing his writing, Mr. Tharp suggests that the student try reading the dream aloud but very quietly to himself. Finally all students seem to be done.)*

Mr. Tharp: Okay? Okay . . . everybody done? Paul? Done? Okay. Now
                . . . would anyone like to share his dream with the rest of
                us?

(*Tentative pause*)

Mr. Tharp: No one? How about you, Tom?

Tom: Well . . . okay . . . Once upon a time I had a dream. . . .
                I had a dream at one time about the prisons. . . . Like Martin
                Luther King I have a dream that one day I will make it to the
                bottom of the mountain. I think I am free because no one can
                stop me from being free at all and nobody gonna free me.
                They may try their best, but they won't get nowhere. The end.

(*Immediate audible response of enthusiasm in the room at the end of the
reading; a scattering of applause that provokes giggles*)

Mr. Tharp: How about another? Jack, do you have anything you want
                to read to us? (*Jack nods "Yes."*) All right.

Jack: I had a dream. I want to be a millionaire. And I want to have
                a free family, and I want to be free. People should have a
                dream because a dream may come true, and I hope that
                everyone had a dream.

Sophie (*without being called on specifically*): "My Dream." One night I
                dreamed that I was a queen and I was having a birthday party
                and then all at once I was looking out the window. You see I
                thought I was crawling on the floor. Then when I got outside,
                I was jumping up and down saying, "I want a rose."

(*A palpable silence holds the class for a moment*)

Mr. Tharp: Another? Fine Merryl.

Merryl: When I was five years old, I dreamed there was a peanuts
                . . . I mean a peanut . . . it was going to get me, and soon
                I woke up and saw that it was only a dream. When I woke
                up my mother about the peanut, she gave me a glass of
                water I asked for.

Mr. Tharp: Atria, do you have a dream to read? Feel free to read it. I
                mean it. Go right ahead.

Atria (*hesitantly*): One night I had a dream that my sister was in the bed
                with me and she was walking around the house with no head.

Maria (*quickly, obviously having gained courage from Atria's reading*):
                One night when I went to bed, I dreamed a . . . that . . .
                that a big dog was after me and I never woke up. I just kept
                on running until I started screaming on my mother's bed.
                My mother thought I had a bad dream.

Harris (*also joining spontaneously when he judged Maria had finished*):
                I had a dream that I was a millionaire and lived on a boat with
                my own studio . . . and I had Batman and Robin on my
                show.

Mr. Tharp (*obviously wooing a small Puerto Rican girl in the back of the room*): Do you have a dream? We'd like to hear from you. Do you have one?

Brenda (*very quietly and hesitantly at first, but increasing vocal intensity as she continues*): Once I had a dream about that I was a horse in a country. My master was Mr. . . . (*name unheard*). He let his friends ride me. Some of his friends were fat. This lady came and asked him can she ride me down the street. My master said yes. She jumped on me, and I took her down the road. I was so tired I jumped and she fell off. On the way back she had to walk.

Mr. Tharp: Maurice, would you like to add yours?

Maurice: Can I sing mine? (*The class responds in mixed fashion; but most students urge him to sing his dream.*) So . . . now . . . everyone listens to my dream. (*He sings the following and accompanies himself on his desk, as if on the bongo drums.*) "This Is Black." Black is not the color of one's skin. It is a state of mind. It is an unyielding desire and fight for freedom and self-determination. It is deep feeling and . . . (*word lost in desk drumming*) We all are people . . . people. . . . It is a love for the lovable regardless of their race or color or religion. It is an understanding and avoidance of the advocate of hatred. It is a deep and sensational expression called soul. It is a knowledge of one's history to build a greater future. Blackness is not the color of one's skin. Are you black?

(*The class applauds spontaneously with enthusiasm.*)

Mr. Tharp: Hey Maurice that was great . . . just great . . . all of you. Wait. Let's try something now. I am going to give you an incomplete thought, and each of you tries to finish it. I mean . . . well . . . if I said, "The leaf falls from the tree like . . ." you would finish the sentence with . . . for instance (*obviously seeking help from the class*). . . .

Merryl: Like gentle rain from heaven?

Mr. Tharp: Great. Another possibility?

Francia (*her first contribution all period*): Like a word that said fall is here. . . .

Mr. Tharp: Yes . . . yes . . . very good . . . exactly . . . okay . . . now . . . Erica, would you go to the board and be our secretary? (*Erica goes*) And I'll give you a beginning. When you think of a way to finish the comparison, the idea, hold up your hand, and let Erica call on you. Be patient so she can write them down. Okay . . . so here it is . . . okay Erica? . . . Okay . . . "A dream deferred is like. . . ."

(*As Erica writes on the board, students whisper and then pause with no response.*)

Mr. Tharp: "A dream deferred is like . . ." any ideas? Raise hands. There. Erica, call on them as you are ready. And let your feelings help. Remember those dreams and that song. Okay.
        . . .

(Hands start going up. Over a period of about twenty minutes, with some further facilitating, the following list was compiled on the blackboards around the room.)

"A dream deferred is like . . ."

1. a meal skipped
2. a sore that festers (*This response provoked laughter, and one student asked Mr. Tharp: "Is that fair? To use the other thing . . . the other poem?" After brief discussion, the class decided to try to be original.*)
* 3. a sky with no sun
* 4. a child without play
* 5. a woman without a man
6. a man without a woman
7. an unpleasant duty
* 8. a "joint" without a match
9. a dreamer's sleep
10. a miscarriage
*11. "I wish I could help!" (*A spontaneous utterance by a student searching in vain for a simile*)
12. an old maid
*13. a smile with no happiness
14. anger without a gun
15. anger with a gun
*16. losing your deferment
*17. trying to put it out of your mind
*18. believing in peace
19. a list without end (*Provided by Erica, humorously; the class laughed and continued.*)
*20. still being hungry
*21. an empty room
22. an impossible wish
*23. a place ya can't go
*24. having nowhere to go
*25. not being able to go
26. being chained and slowly killed
27. opening a beautiful canteloupe and finding the inside rotten (*After this, students were heard to whisper, "What is a canteloupe?" A student explained the fruit with a drawing to those ignorant.*)

28. a Pandora's box (*similar reaction to "Pandora" as to "canteloupe"; explanation followed.*)
*29. reaching out with nothing to touch

Mr. Tharp: Others? Okay . . . great . . . now. . . . Would someone read the whole list so far?

Erica: Let me. Okay?

Mr. Tharp: Fine. Go ahead. (*Erica reads clearly from the board.*) Now, Erica, stay right there. Okay. Now let's vote to see how many of these most of us feel really complete the idea best . . . the idea "A dream deferred is like. . . ." You can vote as many times as you like. Just be sure you vote for ones you really dig . . . those you might have written to express yourself. . . . Dig? Okay. . . .

(*Erica reads each one, and whenever a majority of hands goes up, she places an asterisk, as above, next to the item.*)

Mr. Tharp: Okay. Everyone. Let's see what we've got. Erica, erase the ones we've omitted from the final list. (*She does.*) Now everyone, let's read together what we've written. (*The class, in unison with Erica leading, reads the following.*)

"A dream deferred is like . . ."

a sky with no sun
a child without play

a woman without a man
a "joint" without a match

"I wish I could help!"
a smile with no happiness

losing your deferment
trying to put it out of your mind
believing in peace

still being hungry

an empty room

a place ya can't go
having nowhere to go
not being able to go—

"A dream deferred is like. . ."
reaching out with nothing to touch.

(*The line groupings, punctuation, and reuse of title at end grew out of meaning desired after several unison readings.*)

Mr. Tharp: Well . . . what have we done? What have we got?

Paulette: We've written out our own poem, and I like it better than
            the one about festering. . . (*general sounds of agreement*).
Mr. Tharp: Shall we give it a name? (*Much chatter; spontaneous sug-
            gestions such as "That's Life," "Living," "Hate," and "Bed-
            Stuy"*) No name? Let's vote. How many want to leave it
            the way it is? (*Majority of the hands goes up.*) Okay. We
            don't need a name.
Janet: We can each give it our own name . . . is that okay?
Mr. Tharp: Why not? Okay, let's try reading it. . . .
(*At this point the bell for fire drill interrupts.*)

Having read and evaluated this transcript, what teaching assumptions
do you believe influenced Mr. Tharp's behavior as facilitator at critical
junctures in the class session as recorded in the transcript? In other
words, how does he facilitate the processing of the student input so as to
achieve the most efficient communications system producing the desired
output, the five behavioral objectives?

Here is a numbered list of choices for the following paired paragraphs:

1. ABSOLUTELY prefer Statement *A over* Statement *B.*
2. SOMEWHAT prefer Statement *A over* Statement *B.*
3. ???—absolutely *cannot make any choice* between the two statements.
4. SOMEWHAT prefer Statement *B over* Statement *A.*
5. ABSOLUTELY prefer Statement *B over* Statement *A.*

Indicate your perception of Mr. Tharp's teaching by choosing one of the
two teaching approaches in each of the following pairs; put the appropriate number next to the paragraphs:[2]

A. I know that there is basic material that is so important to the development of interpersonal skills and attitudes that I will do my best to see
   that every student in this class has had contact with these materials
   before this course is over. I know what they need to learn, and they
   will get it. My syllabus is always "ready-to-go," and we always
   follow it.
B. I possess the knowledge and the sensitivity to be able to judge accurately the different needs of the different students in this class.
   Therefore, although I have some structures ready to go, I will have to
   make a lot of decisions en route about the nature of this learning
   experience.

---

[2] These pairs of statements were developed by Theodore Grove for inclusion in
his book on interpersonal communication.

A. A course in skill development, like "Oral Communication," has to give advice and prescribe best-bet behaviors for the students. A basic course like this must serve the immediate needs of students and guide and help them to be able to apply these principles in practical, day-to-day situations that they encounter. I cannot take time to wander off into esoteric material. They are not going to be professionals in communication or teach it—they are going to use it (to communicate), and I must try to give them as much advice and guidance as I can.

B. We prescribed too early in the oral communication classroom and have been trying to live it down ever since. We need to create an awareness of the factors, concepts, and relationships that are operating when people get together to communicate—to be able to describe, analyze, and understand what goes on, whether it is good or bad. We don't know enough about face-to-face communication to prescribe anyway; so we had better avoid "how-to-do-it" attitudes in our teaching.

A. In order to learn anything at all we need to focus inward on ourselves and to assess our reactions, liabilities, assets—to focus on what happens in this classroom laboratory in terms of interpersonal communication. What happens in here is the most relevant data for us and can teach us about ourselves and about our interpersonal communication.

B. We can study and learn about interpersonal communication with more objectivity if we draw examples and data outside of the classroom. We can learn more about interpersonal communication if we first understand how it occurs in groups in which we are not members. Then we can apply this knowledge to groups in which we are members. We are too close to ourselves and our own feelings to separate the relevant from the irrelevant in here and can only make progress as we focus on external instances of interpersonal communication, before anything else.

A. We cannot develop behavioral skills unless we experience the subject matter firsthand. We cannot drive a car by reading about it in the driver's training manual. Nor can we develop interpersonal communication ability by *studying about* that subject from a distance. Total involvement is necessary because in a course with behavioral objectives like this one, intellectual learning must be supplemented by emotional "knowing." This is accomplished through participation and involvement in the subject to be learned.

B. We do not learn anything without acquiring some way of organizing our experience. Raw experience is not necessarily a learning experience—it is quite often a pure waste of time. How can anyone learn about interpersonal communication by just going through the motions of experiencing that which we have already experienced before? What is needed are some conceptual tools (call them theories, concepts, and so forth) to help us analyze and understand the processes that we do experience. We need to create in our students an awareness of the processes of interpersonal communication. Simply engaging in different communication experiences and talking about them is not enough.

Having indicated your perception of Mr. Tharp's teaching, now state your perception of your own teaching by responding to the same pairs of assumptions.

There are no "right" responses to these assumptions; but there are some preferred ones. We have stated our preferences; these preferences are substantiated by student voices. In February 1970[3] the Milwaukee Independent School was established by a group of students, teachers, and parents unwilling to accept the traditional classroom as the only way for education to function. Among the students were "some of the brightest and most successful students in the city's most highly regarded public and private schools. . . ." The student voices proclaimed:

> Too many things are done in school only for the school's purposes and not the students'. There is an extreme lack of respect for students in many schools. Students' initiative and creativity are impeded and inhibited. It [school] is terribly dull, and the kids are pitted against each other for grades and rank in class.
>
> —stated by a boy "who maintained a 95 average"
at a "prestigious" school

> Kids are pumped through the system like products, never learning to think at all.
>
> —stated by a girl who "made A's and B's at
. . . one of Milwaukee's best."

> Here was this nice sterile little cubicle, and you'd turn your mind off when you went inside. When you got out you'd turn it back on. What

[3] William K. Stevens, "Students in Milwaukee Form Their Own School," *The New York Times,* February 13, 1970, p. 34. All subsequent quotations are also from page 34.

went on [in the classroom] has nothing to do with the world, and they
call this learning.

> —stated by a boy when asked to describe
> his senior high school class experience.

Listen to these voices. They are pleading for a system in which the
emphasis is on the processing of human input so that the output will be a
meaningful encounter.

Bibliography

Phase 1

BERLO, DAVID. *The Process of Communication.* New York: Holt, Rinehart and Winston, 1960.

> A classic and simple statement of the behavioristic theories of communication with many examples. This most recent writing in the field of persuasive communication has been influenced by Berlo's ideas.

BORDEN, GEORGE A., RICHARD B. GREGG, and THEODORE G. GROVE. *Speech Behavior and Human Interaction.* Englewood Cliffs, N.J.: Prentice-Hall, 1969.

> Discussion of the theory of human communication in relation to the person in isolation, the interpersonal communication of a small group, and public communication of larger groups. The authors integrate the findings of the psychologist, sociologist, and communications theorist at a very readable level for the beginner in these areas.

BROWN, CHARLES T., and CHARLES VAN RIPER. *Speech and Man.* Englewood Cliffs, N.J.: Prentice-Hall, 1966.

> A popular approach to communication theory with special attention to the role of speech in the development of the self-image and self-acceptance.

CATHCART, ROBERT S., and LARRY SAMOVAR. *Small Group Communication: A Reader.* Dubuque, Ia.: William C. Brown, 1970.

> A selective collection of articles, essays, and research reports that offers the reader an interdisciplinary view of the study of small groups. The editors have placed emphasis on the individual and his role in the group process.

FESSENDEN, SETH A., ROY IVAN JOHNSON, P. MERVILLE LARSON, and KAYE M. GOOD. *Speech for the Creative Teacher.* Dubuque, Ia.: William C. Brown, 1968.

A book designed to help teachers develop listening and speaking skills in students. The focus is on methods and classroom procedures.

MARTIN, HOWARD K., and KENNETH E. ANDERSEN. *Speech Communication: Analysis and Reading*. Rockleigh, N.J.: Allyn-Bacon, 1968.
An anthology of original essays and reprints of research studies in communication, valuable for the summaries of research findings on the nature of communication, strategies, limitations in communication, and the effects of communication. The emphasis is upon purposive human communication.

MILLER, GERALD R. *Speech Communication: A Behavioral Approach*. Indianapolis, Ind.: Bobbs-Merrill, 1966.
An excellent introduction to communication theory with a presentation of communication models and a discussion of "process" in the analysis of communication.

MURRAY, ELWOOD, GERALD M. PHILLIPS, and J. DAVID TRUBY. *Speech: Science-Art*. Indianapolis, Ind.: Bobbs-Merrill, 1969.
A discussion of communication in society with particular emphasis on the needs of the college student in sending and receiving messages.

ROBINSON, KARL F., and ALBERT B. BECKER. *Effective Speech for the Teacher*. New York: McGraw-Hill, 1970.
Instruction for the teacher in developing his own effectiveness in oral communication both in the classroom and in professional contacts outside the classroom.

SCHEIN, EDGAR H., and WARREN G. BENNIS. *Personal and Organizational Change Through Group Methods: The Laboratory Approach*. New York: Wiley, 1965.
Defines the T-group and explains and illustrates the methods of group interaction. The problems in using the approach are presented, and a strong case is made for further research and development of the laboratory method.

SKINNER, B. F. *The Technology of Teaching*. New York: Appleton-Century-Crofts, 1968.
A collection of Skinner's essays on the role of the teacher as a technician of behavior. Skinner presents his view of the classroom as a system of communication.

Phase 2

DEVITO, JOSEPH A. *The Psychology of Speech and Language: Introduction to Psycholinguistics*. New York: Random House, 1970.
Reviews linguistic, learning, and communication theories and applies these insights to the questions of speech and language acquisition,

breakdowns, differences, and effects. The effects chapter deals with attitude change. There is a useful bibliography.

EISENSON, JON, J. JEFFERY AUER, and JOHN V. IRWIN. *The Psychology of Communication.* New York: Appleton-Century-Crofts, 1963.
A summary of the psychology of human interaction including the development of oral communication in the race and the individual communication in the small group, information theory, and the mass media.

MCLUHAN, MARSHALL. *Understanding Media: The Extension of Man.* New York: McGraw-Hill, 1964.
A fascinating integration of many theories of communication with the original thinking of the author. McLuhan's influence has been felt in most recent writing on communication although his ideas are accepted with many qualifications.

MILLER, GEORGE A. *Language and Communication.* New York: McGraw-Hill, 1963.
A scientific and psychological approach to communication elements with chapters on linguistics, psycholinguistics, verbal habits, and the sociology of communication. Miller provides a good summary of early research.

RUESCH, JURGEN, and WELDON KEES. *Nonverbal Communication.* Berkeley: University of California Press, 1961.
An excellent introduction to a subject on which much further research has been done. Still photography is used to illustrate the ways in which people communicate without words. The effects of cultural patterns, movement, object language, and disturbed interaction are presented as a basis for a theoretical statement of nonverbal communication.

SALUS, PETER H. *Linguistics.* Indianapolis, Ind.: Bobbs-Merrill, 1969.
A brief introduction to linguistic analysis of sound systems and generative grammar—valuable as an overview of the subject.

SMITH, ALFRED G. (ed.). *Communication and Culture: Readings in the Code of Human Interaction.* New York: Holt, Rinehart and Winston, 1966.
Mathematical theory, social psychology, and linguistic anthropology integrated in a series of readings to serve as a basis for analysis of syntactics, semantics, and pragmatics. The presentation varies from the technical to a more general presentation of theory.

Phase 3

AGGERT, OTIS J., and ELBERT R. BOWEN. *Communicative Reading.* New York: Macmillan, 1964.
A straightforward consideration of the reader, writer, and listener in the cooperative experience of reading literature aloud. Clear presenta-

tion of a reader's need to control elements of speech for precise conveyance of meaning.

BARATZ, JOAN C. "Language and Cognitive Assessments of Negro Children: Assumptions and Research Needs," *ASHA* (American Speech and Hearing Association), (March 1969), 87–91.

A concise, specific discussion of dialect study with detailed illustration from black speech. There is an excellent list of references for further exploration if desired. Mrs. Baratz is with the Center for Applied Linguistics, 1717 Massachusetts Avenue, N.W., Washington, D.C. The Center has material on dialect study available at cost.

BOLESLAVSKY, RICHARD. *Acting: The First Six Lessons.* New York: Theatre Arts, 1969.

Demonstrates the nature and importance of concentration in the creative and recreative act. Boleslavsky's advice to an aspiring actress distills the complexity of human behavior.

CUMMINGS, E. E. *I: Six Non-Lectures.* New York: Atheneum, 1968.

Provides the reader with a vivid illustration of what creativity can be like. The American poet talks about himself—his life and his poetry—and includes selections of his own favorites from literature.

FRIES, CHARLES CARPENTER. *Teaching and Learning English as a Foreign Language.* Ann Arbor: University of Michigan Press, 1956.

An invaluable analysis of the sounds, structures, and words of English for a native's better understanding of English and a scientific approach to classroom work with dialects.

JOOS, MARTIN. *The Five Clocks.* New York: Harcourt Brace Jovanovich, 1967.

A practical consideration of the styles of English usage that avoids the traps encountered when using traditional, often inaccurate labels such as "formal," "colloquial," and "substandard" for usage.

LADO, ROBERT. *Language Teaching: A Scientific Approach.* New York: McGraw-Hill, 1964.

A detailed treatment of language teaching—native as well as foreign—from sound system in spoken English to programmed learning and teaching machines. It is useful as a scientific guide in understanding one's native language when dealing with dialects.

———. *Communication Barriers for the Culturally Deprived.* 1966.

A cooperative research project conducted by Raven I. McDavid, J. and William M. Austin. This study, with contributions by leaders in the area of dialect, includes examination of dialects of Chicago. It has a useful bibliography. For additional studies of this sort, consult the Cooperative Research Program of the Office of Education, U.S. Department of Health, Education, and Welfare, Washington, D.C.

PARRISH, WAYLAND MAXFIELD. *Reading Aloud.* New York: Ronald Press, 1966.
A careful examination of how to project the meaning of poetry and prose
when read aloud for listeners' comprehension. Parrish is particularly
helpful for the reader working for accuracy of an author's "attitude."

Phase 4

ASHTON-WARNER, SYLVIA. *Teacher.* New York: Simon and Schuster, 1963;
Bantam, 1965.
An account by Miss Ashton-Warner on how an inspired teacher, here
working with the Maori children in New Zealand, can make the classroom—her "infant room"—into a life space for "organic" learning and
spontaneous creativity. Reading and dancing, and all other activities,
spring from the same provocative seminal source.

HOLT, JOHN. *How Children Fail.* New York: Delta, 1964.
A close look by Holt, in diary form, at his actual students as human
beings, as individuals, with specific needs for life. He works to discover
how to help his students realize their needs.

———. *How Children Learn.* New York: Pitman, 1967.
Concentrates on the very young child and demonstrates how meaningful
spontaneous practice supersedes traditional theorizing and the security
of a classroom structure more important to the insecure adult than the
learning student.

JOHNSON, WENDELL. *Your Most Enchanted Listener.* New York: Harper & Row,
1956.
Provides useful analysis of speaking and listening for "your most enchanted listener": yourself. The author was a foremost teacher of speech
and himself a stutterer.

LEONARD, GEORGE B. *Education and Ecstasy.* New York: Delta, 1968.
Examines the destructive folly of traditional education, warns of its
current dangers, but suggests an alternative for the needs of our technological society, drawing on schools already functioning. Leonard helps
us reexamine our roles—student and teacher—with an understanding
of teacher as facilitator in a creative learning experience.

LIBARLE, MARC and TOM SELIGSON (eds.). *The High School Revolutionaries.*
New York: Random House, 1970.
Twenty-two essays by students of private and public school demanding
change in education—by violence if need be. This book is a realistic
national sampling of youthful voices edited by young and receptive
minds.

MEARNS, HUGHES. *Creative Power: The Education of Youth in the Creative
Arts.* New York: Dover, 1968.

Demonstrates from the author's own experience how previously threatened, defensive students can be helped to discover and develop their
own creative potential.

POSTMAN, NEIL, and CHARLES WEINGARTNER. *Teaching as a Subversive Activity*. New York: Delacorte, 1969.
Methodically debunks the mechanically maintained traditions of mass
American education, isolates modern needs for students and teachers,
and suggests a way to survival. The authors include numerous useful
quotations.

SHUY, ROGER W. *Discovering American Dialects*. National Council of Teachers
of English, 508 South Sixth Street, Champaign, Illinois, 61820. 1967.
A concise, specific consideration of dialect as a geographic and social
phenomenon. It contains useful, clear diagrams and illustrative examples.

———— (ed.). *Social Dialects and Language Learning*. National Council of
Teachers of English, 508 South Sixth Street, Champaign, Illinois, 61822.
1964.
A 1964 conference report featuring articles by Raven I. McDavid, Jr.,
William A. Stewart, Lee A. Pederson, Albert H. Marckwardt, and other
leaders in the field discussing various aspects of dialect study and teaching.

SPOLIN, VIOLA. *Improvisation for the Theater*. Evanston, Illinois: Northwestern
University Press, 1963.
A "handbook" that takes student and teacher on a developmental course
from basic sensory exercises to intricate group participation activities.
This is a basic book in the understanding of concentration as a key to
human communication.

STANISTREET, GRACE M. *teaching is a dialogue*. Childrens Centre for Creative
Arts, Adelphi University, Garden City, N. Y., 1969.
A distillation, in letter form to approximate the "dialogue" of learning, of
Miss Stanistreet's philosophy and techniques in considering communication the cycle of initiation, response, initiation. It includes materials
ranging from basic sensory games to group improvisational games and is
a basic book in the understanding of concentration as a key to human
communication.

Index